Meant for Heaven

a little girl's journey to paradise

Meant for Heaven

a little girl's journey to paradise

Bryan Young

CFI
An Imprint of Cedar Fort, Inc.
Springville, Utah

ISBN 13: 978-1-4621-1985-1

Published by CFI, an imprint of Cedar Fort, Inc.
2373 W. 700 S., Springville, UT 84663
Distributed by Cedar Fort, Inc., www.cedarfort.com

Library of Congress Cataloging-in-Publication data on file

Cover design by Shawnda T. Craig
Cover design © 2017 by Cedar Fort, Inc.
Edited and typeset by Rebecca Bird

Printed in the United States of America

10 9 8 7 6 5 4 3 2 1

Printed on acid-free paper

To my dear wife, Aleta, and my children,
Holland, Dallin, Nelson, and Hinckley, for walking beside me
on this journey through life.
And to my parents, Pam and Kent, for teaching me to trust in
the Lord through good times and bad.

Contents

Contents

Introduction

We interact with hundreds of people every day, and those people interact with even more people. Think about your average day. You might wake up and greet your immediate family members or roommates.

Now think about when you leave your house and go into your neighborhood. Each house is filled with people waking up to their own days. As you get into your car and hit the road, every vehicle you pass carries people with their own unique stories and experiences.

When you arrive at work, human interaction begins with your fellow employees, your clients, and your boss. Each person in your office has a unique story to tell.

I say this because the story that follows could be anyone's story. Maybe you or a loved one have experienced something similar. In reality, there are people all around us who are struggling with their own pain and trials, and many times, we never know.

Though my experience is unique to me, I hope it resonates with you, because no one is free of trials. We've each had many moments where we've felt overwhelmed by our lot in life. That's why I share this story now, not only to help you through your trials, but so you might better empathize with the many people you meet each day dealing with illnesses such as cancer or the death of a loved one.

This is an account of my experience raising my daughter, an extraordinary little girl named Holland Young.

My life was full of unique experiences that helped me to grow and develop as a person long before Holland was born, but the events of her life shaped me in a way that nothing else ever had.

I originally wrote this account for my own personal records so that I could go back and recall what happened to me and to show Holland what happened to her as she got older and would most likely forget these things. However, after Holland died, I felt prompted to finish these records so that I could share them with my family, especially my other children. And as I kept putting it off, I felt more strongly that I needed to finish it by the second anniversary of Holland's death. When I finished it, I felt prompted to share it with my friends and family on Facebook. Then I started to feel prompted to send it to random acquaintances and old friends. I then felt prompted to share it with strangers on online message boards.

I never wanted to publish this story—that was not my intent in writing it. Many people have told me that the sacred moments that I describe in this book need to be kept to myself. While I do believe sacred experiences should not be shared lightly, I only feel comfortable sharing this with you because I have felt prompted by the Lord to do so. I pray that as you read these words and experiences they will help you. I pray that you will appreciate how sacred and personal these experiences are to me and to my family. That being said, as you feel prompted, please share this story with those who may come to mind as you read it. I know that these words will help many people through their own trials and I hope that you will be one of those people.

Who Am I and Who Is Holland?

My name is Bryan Young and my wife's name is Aleta. We met at Brigham Young University (BYU) in Provo, Utah, in 2004. I

Introduction

had just gotten home from my Latter-day Saint mission in Boise, Idaho, and we met while living in the same apartment complex. I was born and raised in Virginia in a suburb of Washington, DC. Aleta Grant was from Washington, just outside of Seattle. We dated for a short time before we were married in April of 2005. We were a young couple at BYU living the BYU dream as poor married students. We both graduated in 2007 with our bachelors degrees. She majored in geography and I majored in psychology. I stayed at BYU to continue my education and enrolled in the school psychology advanced masters program that fall, while Aleta worked full-time at an Internet company.

As married BYU students, we often felt the pressure to start our family. However, after making it a matter of consistent prayer and temple attendance, we felt that we needed to wait until we had good and consistent insurance, since Aleta planned to stay at home with our children. So we waited until right before I started my internship with the Provo School District, and after three years of marriage, Aleta was finally pregnant.

We were very excited to find out that we were starting our family with a little girl. As excited as I was, there was certainly some trepidation at the prospect of welcoming a new life into the world. One day while Aleta was at work and I was getting ready to go to class, I was listening to the weekly BYU devotional. This particular week Elder Jeffrey R. Holland gave the devotional entitled, "Remember Lot's Wife: Faith Is for the Future." As a young husband on the verge of becoming a new father, the following quote stuck out to me:

> I remember one fall day—I think it was in the first semester after our marriage in 1963—we were walking together up the hill past the Maeser Building on the sidewalk that led between the President's Home and the Brimhall Building. Somewhere on that path we stopped and wondered what we had gotten ourselves into. Life that day seemed so overwhelming, and the undergraduate plus graduate years that we still anticipated before us seemed monumental, nearly insurmountable. Our love for each other and our commitment to the gospel were

strong, but most of all the other temporal things around us seemed particularly ominous.

On a spot that I could probably still mark for you today, I turned to Pat and said something like this: "Honey, should we give up? I can get a good job and carve out a good living for us. I can do some things. I'll be okay without a degree. Should we stop trying to tackle what right now seems so difficult to face?"

In my best reenactment of Lot's wife, I said, in effect, "Let's go back. Let's go home. The future holds nothing for us."

Then my beloved little bride did what she has done for forty-five years since then. She grabbed me by the lapels and said, "We are not going back. We are not going home. The future holds *everything* for us."[1]

This idea stuck out to me so strongly, and any fear that I had of being an unprepared father vanished in the idea that "the future holds everything." This talk from Elder Holland was so striking that when Aleta got home, I told her I liked the idea of naming our little girl Holland. After months of debating back and forth we each made our final list of names with Holland at the top of both of our lists. We looked at each other and said, "I think we just named our daughter." And so we named our first child after a great man, an Apostle of the Lord (a trend we have continued with our other children).

On May 13, 2009, we welcomed Holland Gwen Young into the world, our family, and our hearts. As Holland began to learn and grow, she always hit her developmental milestones early, starting with the moment when she rolled over at two weeks. She started crawling at five months, walking at nine months, coherently talking at seventeen months, potty training at twenty months, and memorizing full stories when she was two years old. If there was something to do, Holland did it. She got the most out of each second of her life. She was always full of energy—for good and bad. Holland's signature expression was always bright-eyed, her mouth wide open in excitement. No matter how

mundane the event, she would enthusiastically jump up and down to cheer the moment.

Holland had a strong will and personality in the good times and the bad. Beyond simple toddler misbehaviors and battle of wills, Holland was known to really dig in her heels. While every kid might do things like color on the doors and walls, not every kid will wipe their poop on the walls to spite their parents. But she could also make us laugh and melt our hearts with just a look. Her strong personality that she had developed would help her in the trials that lay ahead for her.

The following is a record of the events that have surrounded our experiences with her battle with cancer. Although she has many entertaining and engaging stories from her earlier years, this story will focus on the fourteen months following her third birthday. I record not only the events, but also our emotions and the spiritual lessons we learned. Although this time in our lives was a great trial, we never want to forget the lessons we learned. It is our hope that by sharing these experiences, we will become better people and help others grow in their faith as well.

Notes

1. Jeffrey R. Holland, "Remember Lot's Wife: Faith Is for the Future" (Brigham Young University devotional, January 13, 2009), speeches.byu.edu.

1

"Daddy, My Head Hurts"

For her third birthday in May of 2013, Holland had a very big party. One of my good friends was a professional clown, and he agreed to do a show for Holland and all of her friends. It was a lot of fun and Holland loved every moment of it. I remember the way her face lit up as she unwrapped a simple dollar-store purple jump rope—the only present she requested. Her friends and family gave her movies, books, art supplies, and even some swords and a light saber. (She loved everything, including princesses, football, zombies, and Jedis.) It was an ideal third birthday party.

But despite this, at one point I couldn't find Holland anywhere. We began looking for her, though she would rarely run off like this. A friend claimed to have seen her go out the front door, so I ran outside and chased her down around the corner of our house. "Holland! What are you doing? What about your birthday party?" She responded that she wanted to go and play with the butterflies. She had a room full of friends, presents, and even a magical clown, but she wanted to be alone playing with butterflies. Though I didn't know it at the time, this experience foreshadowed what was coming in the months ahead: as everyone else worried for her and panicked, she would make a journey all by herself.

Soon after her birthday, Holland told me, "Daddy, my head hurts."

She continued to be bothered by headaches for several days. At first we thought this might have been the result of banging heads with a friend or hitting her head on some furniture a few weeks earlier.

However, the headaches began to intensify to the point that they were waking her up at night. She also began to throw up in the morning, which prompted us to take her to our family pediatrician, Dr. Ryan. Though she wasn't feverish, Holland's symptoms persisted for about a week.

The doctor expressed concern, but he advised us to take her home and continue to give her Tylenol for the pain. He said if the symptoms hadn't gone away within a few days, we should bring her back in to schedule a magnetic resonance imaging (MRI).

The medicine didn't help, and the pain continued to keep Holland up every night. We all got between two and four hours of very interrupted sleep each night.

One night, after staying up with Holland for several hours, I felt prompted to give her a priesthood blessing of healing. I placed my hands on her head and felt guided to say she would be healed and able to sleep again.

She woke up again about an hour later, and I prayed for a confirmation of this blessing. The Lord told me she would be able to get the rest she needed by Thursday. This was Tuesday night, so I anticipated two more nights of her suffering, and then it would all be a distant memory.

But Holland continued to struggle sleeping and began to throw up more regularly in the mornings and at night. Thursday came and went, and by Friday she was even worse. I started to doubt the effectiveness of my blessing and the power of the Lord to heal her.

Though her pain lessened over Memorial Day weekend, the day after, her symptoms were back and even stronger than before. She threw up four times that morning, and Aleta and I decided it was time to follow the pediatrician's recommendation to get an

Chapter 1

MRI. As we scheduled the appointment, Aleta hugged and held Holland, who was unnaturally still and quiet.

We took Holland in the following day for her three-year checkup, and Dr. Ryan explained that her symptoms indicated the possibility of hydrocephalus, a tumor, or simply a pesky virus. He said he would call us with the MRI results the day after, and if the results were troubling, we could visit with him that day and discuss the next step.

When she woke up the next morning, Holland was feeling pretty good. She asked us if she could go to the park, but we told her we could only go if she was feeling fine. We believe that the Lord knew she needed to do one more fun thing before she ended up in the hospital, so she was blessed that day to not throw up or have a headache.

As I had just gotten off work for the summer, I had the time to take her to the park near our house. We had a fun time playing together on the playground, and it was a wonderfully "normal" day.

That afternoon we headed up to Riverton for the MRI. This was our first glimpse of what a fighter Holland was. When they tried to sedate her, it took longer than normal to get her to sleep, and we later found out she had awoken during the MRI and needed an extra dose of medicine to get her back to sleep.

We went to the recovery room where my parents joined us. Soon the MRI tech carried Holland into the room. She was in and out of consciousness with her eyes closed, and she was crying. The tech put her in Aleta's arms, and then the whirlwind started.

A social worker came in with a nurse, who told us we would be getting a call from our pediatrician. Less than three seconds later, the phone rang. The doctor said there was an abnormality in Holland's scans and that we needed to immediately check in at the emergency room at Primary Children's Hospital in Salt Lake City and meet with Dr. Burkes.

The sudden change of events was disorienting, and the social worker tried to prepare us while we waited for Holland to wake up enough to get in the car. We had already been told by Dr. Ryan that a tumor was a possibility, so we were mentally prepared for the news, but we were struggling emotionally as the reality and severity of the situation started to sink in. Three-year-olds don't get tumors.

Primary Children's Hospital

After nearly an hour, Holland was stable enough to move, so we began the trip to Primary Children's Hospital—a journey that would become all too familiar over the next year. My mom came with us to help us navigate our way there, and Aleta called her mom to give her an update. As she began to tell her the news, Aleta became overwhelmed and began to cry so hard she couldn't speak. I took the phone and told Aleta's mom that we were on our way to the hospital and we would call her back after we talked to the doctors.

The usual thirty-minute drive from the Riverton clinic to the hospital turned into an hour due to rush hour traffic, and Holland fell asleep again. When we finally arrived and checked Holland into the ER, Holland had woken up and was crying loudly; we couldn't get her to calm down. We were eventually allowed into a back room where we were introduced to our new friend—the "Holland Movie Channel." Holland quieted as we settled in and watched the Disney movie *Tangled.*

We eventually met with Dr. Lee, who explained that Dr. Burkes had already gone home for the day. She pulled up the MRI and showed us that Holland had both a tumor about the size of a golf ball and an equally large cyst on the outer left part of her cerebellum.

She also showed us that the tumor had put pressure on her fourth ventricle, which had not allowed her cerebrospinal fluid (CSF) to drain. This had caused her other ventricles to expand and to put added pressure on her brain, which had caused Holland's headaches and vomiting.

Dr. Lee explained that we would not know the nature of the tumor until they were able to take a biopsy, so she scheduled a surgery for the next afternoon. Though Holland would need to stay in the hospital overnight in preparation for it, she was allowed to eat, which was great news since she'd been fasting all morning. She was put on a steroid to reduce the swelling in her brain and to help ease her headaches.

By this time, other family members had arrived, and we shed many tears as we faced the risks and realities that brain surgery brought. But we were happy that, for the moment, Holland was feeling better and enjoying her new cool hospital jammies.

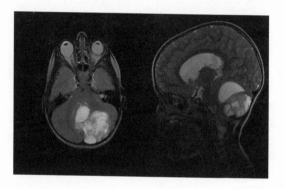

2

The Long Drive Home

When they told us the news about Holland's tumor, I just kind of took it all in. It was a numb, hazy feeling. It felt surreal, like some kind of weird dream. I heard what they were saying, but I didn't fully process through what this would mean for the future, what all this would mean for our family and the life of our little girl. I heard every word but my mind couldn't see pass the moment right in front of me, which was getting this little girl to feel happy again. Now that the medicine was helping Holland, she was happy, and the doctors had a plan, I was ready to leave.

We hadn't anticipated an overnight stay in Salt Lake City, so Aleta stayed with Holland that night in the hospital while I drove home to get the things we needed for the coming week. The next morning I also had a follow-up doctor's appointment scheduled in Provo for a finger I'd broken a month earlier. Leaving my daughter and my wife, who was eight months pregnant, in the hospital while I drove home to sleep in my own bed was hard.

The toughest part, though, was the drive back to Provo alone in the middle of the night. In the quiet, all the thoughts that my mind couldn't process while in the hospital now all but consumed me. I cried the whole way home, dwelling on the fact we could lose Holland and the unfairness of the situation. I thought,

Meant for Heaven

Why can't this be happening to me instead of this little girl who has so much life ahead of her?

I turned up the radio to block out these thoughts, but the lyrics to each song hit me like a ton of bricks. "And you feel like falling down, I'll carry you home tonight."[1] All I could think was, *Holland's falling down, and I can't carry her home tonight.* "When she was just a girl she expected the world, but it flew away from her reach"[2] *All of Holland's dreams and expectations are flying out of her reach.* I couldn't block out these thoughts that life would never be the same.

Each thought kept pulling me down into the abyss, and I was overwhelmed with the reality that she might die and there was nothing I could do about it. I felt that we as a family had been dealt with unfairly. She was so innocent and yet she was being punished. I felt helpless, I felt angry, I felt sad, I felt despair like never before. I didn't want to lose her, but I felt that my faith could no longer help me. I had been faithful to the Church and to God my whole life. I had served a mission, married in the temple, and faithfully served in presidencies and bishoprics. I had done everything God had asked me to do and this was how He had repaid me. These dark clouds filled my mind the whole ride home.

When I finally arrived, I couldn't sleep. I was too upset and angry. I tried to pray to God, but all that came out was, "Why? Why? Why? Why is this happening to her? Why couldn't I heal her?"

I had given her multiple priesthood blessings, and I couldn't understand why Holland wasn't getting better. Didn't I have enough faith? Was God punishing me?

Then a dark question crossed my mind: *Is God even real at all?*

Why would a loving God do this to my daughter? It was a long restless night. But then I realized that in order to be there for her, I needed to find peace with all of these questions swirling around in my head. I could not help her and be the rock that she would need me to be if I wasn't at peace with myself.

Chapter 2

After a terrible night of these dreadful thoughts, I went to the Provo Utah Temple at 7:00 a.m. I knew I needed to talk to the Lord. I could not go on with this cognitive dissonance in my head. I needed God to explain *why* this was happening or I would conclude that God was not real. Simply put, if He would not help me out now, when I needed Him most, then I wouldn't be able to believe that He even existed anymore. I explained my situation to a worker there, telling him that my daughter had just been diagnosed with a brain tumor and that I needed to talk to the Lord and ask Him why. My tears were thick through this explanation, and this temple worker, with great love and compassion in his eyes, had me change into my temple clothes and then escorted me up to the celestial room.

I found a chair, closed my eyes, and bowed my head. Tears again filled my eyes as I asked the Lord, "Why is this happening? Why couldn't I heal her? Why her and not me? *Why?*"

A moment later the words of the Lord filled my mind and heart with such power that I could not doubt the source of these thoughts. I was startled and further knew they were not my own thoughts because these were not words of comfort at first. The Lord chastised me and told me that the priesthood is not mine to do with it what I want. It is the Lord's power to be used to bring to pass His will, not mine.

He also taught me that I needed to have my faith in Him and His Son, not in the outcomes that I wanted. If things did not go as I planned, then *my* plan was flawed, not the Lord's. I learned that if we truly desire to become like our Father in Heaven, He cannot simply remove the trials in front of us. We need to learn from these experiences and grow stronger through them. I needed to trust in Him regardless of what happened during the surgery or going forward. He would not leave me. And now, I would not leave Him.

I left the temple, went to my appointment, and then headed back to the hospital with such great peace that though Holland might die, it would be okay because Christ had overcome death and she would live again. I also had a new faith in the power of the temple sealing that regardless of the outcome with her surgery, we would live together forever.

I thought it was interesting that the Lord never told me that she would live; He just said that things would work out. I knew that this experience would allow us to draw closer as a family and closer to the Lord. I now know that if the Lord had healed her when I gave her a blessing in her bedroom, we never could have shared our knowledge of the power of the Atonement with as many as people as we have. The peace that I felt was able to not only give me solace to my questions, but also allow me to be strong for her during the hard road ahead.

Meanwhile, Back at the Hospital

While I was down in Provo, Aleta stayed with Holland for her first night in the hospital. Aleta was thirty-three weeks pregnant with Dallin, so sleeping on a hospital couch was not ideal for restful sleep. All in all, Holland and Aleta got about two hours of sleep that night. We would all have a hard time sleeping in this new environment with lights flashing on monitors and nurses coming in every couple of hours.

The next morning, Aleta and Holland woke up around 6:00 a.m. Aleta later told me, "I've heard people say that angels roam the halls of Primary Children's Hospital, and many times throughout our experience there I have felt that to be true. That first night and next day, I believe angels helped our little family."

Being so far along in her pregnancy, Aleta shouldn't have been able to get through that day with so little sleep, but a combination of prayers, angels, and adrenaline helped her. Early that next morning, she met Dr. Burkes for the first time. He came in with a few of the residents and asked some questions about Holland's symptoms. The conversation lasted maybe five minutes. She told me, "It was weird to think that later that day he would be performing surgery on our daughter. I really knew nothing about him, but yet I had to trust him that he'd be able to get the tumor out."

Chapter 2

Since Dr. Burkes had two other surgeries scheduled ahead of us that day, we didn't know when Holland would be going in for surgery. This meant she had to fast all day to be ready to go in at a moment's notice. I joined Aleta later that morning and helped distract Holland from the fact that she couldn't have any food.

About an hour before she went in for surgery, she was starving and nothing we did could distract her from it. We tried to keep her comfortable as she pleaded with us for food, and it broke my heart.

Finally the nurses came to take Holland into the operating room. We met with the anesthesiologist for a few minutes, and then kissed our little girl good-bye.

Notes

1. Fun, "We Are Young," Sony/ATV Music Publishing LLC and Warner/Chappell Music,Inc., 2012.
2. Coldplay, "Paradise," written by William Champion, Christopher Anthony John Martin, Jonathan Mark Buckland, Brian Eno, and Guy Rupert Berryman (Peermusic Publishing and Universal Music Publishing Group, 2011).

3

The Surgeries Begin

We waited with my parents in the surgery waiting room during the five-hour-long surgery. A nurse called every hour or so to give us updates during the surgery, and then Dr. Burkes met with us when it was completed. He told us that Holland had tolerated the surgery well and that he was 99 percent sure he had gotten it all out.

He told us the tumor looked like a juvenile pilocytic astrocytoma (JPA), and we said, "A what?"

He told us that it was a grade 1 tumor and that if we had to pick a type of brain tumor, this would be the one to pick. We all let out a huge sigh of relief. I felt grateful that we had received the best news possible, given the situation. We waited about a half hour longer as they finished stitching her up, and then we were allowed to go see her in the pediatric intensive care unit (PICU).

When we entered the room, she looked so sad—miserable, tired, and disoriented. She had no idea what had just happened to her. Her arms were in braces because she had tried to pull out the tube that was draining excess CSF from around her brain. Although she was miserable, she also looked pretty cute because they had put her hair in pigtails. But it was only cute until we saw the giant five-inch scar going up the back of her neck and

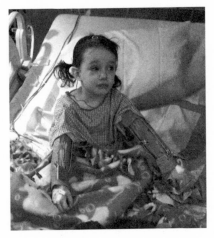

head. It was closed with thick, black nylon stitches, and her hair was shaved around it.

Holland was pretty upset about the braces, so we explained that she couldn't pull on the tube on the top of her head. She agreed, and the nurse let us take the braces off.

Even though the surgery was for her benefit, I felt terrible and guilty. We had told her that the doctor would help make her headaches go away, then we sent her off, and she came back in more pain with tubes sticking out of her. All she wanted was for us to rub her back—it was the only thing that would comfort her. She wouldn't move her neck at all since it was so stiff and caused her so much pain from the surgery, so sleep that night was pretty difficult for us all.

The next day, Holland had a full MRI of her head, neck, and spine. The procedure typically takes about ninety minutes, but it took about two hours with Holland because they had such a difficult time keeping her sedated. Despite the drugs, she wasn't falling asleep, so they gave her another dose. Then, when she fell asleep, she stopped breathing. So they gave her some oxygen, but that woke her up again. This went back and forth a couple of times, and finally they added another drug to get her knocked out, but still breathing.

The results of the MRI came back with both good news and bad news. Good news: the tumor had not spread down her spine or anywhere else in her brain. Bad news: there was still tumor in her cerebellum.

Although Dr. Burkes had been "99 percent sure" he had gotten it all out, he explained that the brain matter was under such pressure that when you start taking the tumor out, the matter starts to fill in and morph, making it difficult to locate the entire tumor.

What was left was pretty much the rind, similar to the rind of an orange, with just the outer pieces on both sides. It was our first defeat in this fight. But the doctor explained that since this type of tumor was benign, it shouldn't come back if he got it all out. So the second surgery was scheduled for Monday morning.

Sunday at the Hospital

We were able to leave the PICU and head back to the neuroscience trauma unit (NTU). Holland again had a rough night sleeping. The next morning was Sunday and Aleta brought my church clothes so that I could go to the church service at the hospital.

Aleta stayed with Holland while I went to the sacrament service, which happened to be a fast and testimony meeting. If you ever feel sorry for yourself or overwhelmed by your problems, go to the sacrament meeting at Primary Children's Hospital. The congregation was filled with doctors and nurses as well as families with their children. Some children had IVs and were wearing hospital gowns, while others were dressed up but had obviously been ravaged by the effects of chemo.

I felt a need to bear my testimony of the lessons I had learned in the temple. I also wanted to tell about the dark place I had been when I questioned for a brief moment the existence of God, and how He quickly returned to my side when I was able to humble myself and accept His will.

I then listened to the words of other families that shared experiences of long bouts with cancer, as well as the miraculous experience of a father who watched his son drown and die but then come back to life under the care of these doctors. It left me with an understanding that trials are an opportunity to trust in God, as these families had done.

The outcomes for some of these children were not optimistic, but they still had hope and faith in the Lord. These people had faith that God would care for them and that the Atonement and the priesthood were real. They understood that this life is temporary for us all.

I talked with the hospital's branch president after the sacrament service, and he agreed to send a Primary lesson for Holland. He also said he and his counselors would come down and talk with us. Soon some sisters came to teach Holland a Primary lesson. She was grumpy and didn't like people coming into her room, but these sweet sisters sang a song and taught Holland a brief lesson. It was a nice sense of normalcy during this crazy whirlwind time.

Later that evening, two members of the branch presidency came to visit our family. They thanked me for my words in the testimony meeting and asked if they could do anything for us. We mentioned that Aleta had been having contractions since our time in the hospital, and they offered to assist me in giving her a priesthood blessing.

In the blessing, the Lord promised Aleta that she would be able to have no complications with her labor and pregnancy and that the baby would be blessed to have a peaceful spirit that would comfort us through our trials. The Spirit also confirmed at this point that our baby should indeed be named Dallin, the name I had received about a month previously in the temple. The blessing brought a sense of peace again to our family that we would be able to make it through this ordeal.

My parents again came to spend time with us in the hospital that night. They were a great source of support and comfort throughout our stay there. Holland enjoyed playing with a set of stacking rings and made up her own game called "Ring the Gack" (loosely based on the little story in the Dr. Seuss book *One Fish, Two Fish, Red Fish, Blue Fish*[1]). The game consisted of throwing the rings on the ground for one of us to pick up.

She also had fun making "donut eyes" with the rings as well. It was nice to see her being silly and happy. Aleta went back to my parents' house, and I prepared for another restless night by Holland's side. This room had a couch, which was more comfortable than the pull-out chair in the PICU, but Holland was still very uncomfortable, so for much of the night I stayed beside her in the hospital bed with her head propped up against my arm so she didn't have to lay against the stitches on the back of her head. We watched "Holland Movies" most of the night as we both struggled to get sleep.

The Second Surgery

In the morning, Aleta returned to the hospital and numerous doctors came in to prepare us for the surgery that was scheduled for later that afternoon. Holland began to struggle again with another day of fasting for her upcoming surgery.

My parents rejoined us as we again waited during the five-hour-long surgery, and Bishop May from our home ward unexpectedly came to visit us. He shared some of his experiences of dealing with tumors, and we were comforted to know that he was praying for us and was making sure we had the things we needed.

At the end of the surgery, Dr. Burkes came to talk with us in the waiting room and said that she did okay during the surgery, although she had lost a bit of blood and had needed a transfusion. He said that with the pressure gone, everything had kind of settled and he was able to go right in and see exactly where the tumor was. We were happy with the relatively good news and were anxious for the other doctors to finish sewing her up so we could see her.

When we were finally able to see her, we could tell that her body was certainly more exhausted. Her skin was the palest I had ever seen it, and I knew it was going to be another rough night. I ended up having to cradle Holland's head in my arms and watch the movie *Flushed Away* on repeat five times, since she would go in and out of sleep and would be upset when she missed certain parts of the movie.

She had progressively gotten more ornery as this experience wore on, and she was now starting to growl at nurses and doctors that came to check on her. She had also started using the excuse that she needed to go potty in order to delay doing things—something she continued to do the rest of the time in the hospital. She was wearing a pull-up diaper, but she refused to go until she was able to get up and go like a big girl.

Holland was supposed to have another MRI the next morning to make sure the tumor was gone, so she was fasting again. But there was a miscommunication between the staff members, and the MRI was never ordered. We were told the procedure wouldn't happen until 5:00 p.m., which meant she would have to fast all day again. We were extremely upset by this news, and told the nurse there was no way we were going to make her wait that long! Holland had only eaten three meals in five days due to all the surgeries and procedures.

The nurse understood that we were upset and made a series of calls to see if he could bump up the appointment. Finally, they were able to get her in at 11:00 a.m.

Later that afternoon as Holland was resting, Dr. Burkes came to talk to us about the latest MRI. He said there was still one piece left, about the size of a pinky-finger tip. We were crushed and heartbroken, and Dr. Burkes was extremely disappointed as well. This tiny piece of tumor was tucked behind a portion of brain matter. He said he could schedule surgery again the next day, but we knew we couldn't do that—Holland was beaten up too badly. She needed to heal, and we needed to see her as her regular three-year-old spunky, happy self.

Dr. Burkes told us that we could wait a few months. There was a 33 percent chance the tumor would grow bigger, 33 percent chance it would stay the same size, and 33 percent chance that it would shrink and be absorbed by the body.

We immediately knew we should wait. We wanted to take the less invasive route, and we would spend the entire summer praying that it would miraculously go away. Holland needed time to heal and get back to her regular life before we shook things up again and added baby Dallin to the family.

Notes

1. Dr. Seuss, *One Fish, Two Fish, Red Fish, Blue Fish* (New York: Random House, 1960), 58.

4

Recovery Time

The next couple of days we poured salt over all of Holland's food. Her sodium levels were too low—apparently three meals in five days and a blood transfusion was too much stress on a tiny three-year-old body. My coworker Brad kindly brought her a chicken nugget Happy Meal for her first meal after the second surgery, along with a giant sun balloon. She loved it! Better yet,

she immediately perked up after eating. The color came back to her cheeks and her lips, and a smile returned to her face. She'd always been serious about food and she had been fasting for so long that this food was an amazing treat.

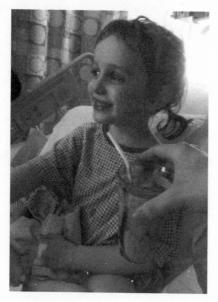

The doctors had prescribed a sodium solution as well, but it tasted terrible. We tried to sneak it into whatever she ate, but Holland started to figure us out. We gave her chocolate shakes (which had the highest sodium content offered at the hospital) and sprinkled extra table salt on everything. Before too long, Holland's sodium levels were back to normal, and she was cleared to go home.

Before we left the hospital, we had the great opportunity to have BYU's mascot, Cosmo the Cougar, visit us in the hospital. We had put in a request on Facebook to have Cosmo come see Holland in the hospital. I found out that Shawn Watkins, a young man who had been in the LDS singles ward I served in, was the guy in the Cosmo suit.

Shawn gave me a call and said the publicity people at the hospital had approved his visit, and he would be able to visit Holland before we left for home. Unfortunately, when he arrived, Holland had just woken up from a nap and was very grumpy. She cried most of the time that Cosmo was there.

I felt bad about it, because Shawn and another friend from the singles ward were very kind to come cheer her up. We really appreciated it though, and looking back at that experience, Holland was really grateful for and excited about the picture he signed for her.

We soon headed home and tried to get back into a normal routine. The next morning, Holland got up, had breakfast, and then wanted to help with the dishes. We knew she was back to her old self, if not a little bit better.

But we were still a long way from normal. Holland was receiving steroids as part of her treatment to help reduce the swelling, and we were new to the world of steroids. We discovered that "roid rage" was one of the side effects of taking so many steroids. Holland would become uncharacteristically angry at times, and she was always hungry. She would eat three or four servings of a meal, and about an hour later she'd want a snack.

She would also get very emotional and cry when things didn't go her way, which was unusual for her. So we took things easy and watched a lot of movies on the couch. Luckily, once we got her stitches out and finished the steroid treatments, Holland was nearly herself again. Within two weeks our lives were back to normal, and we began to hope and pray that the tumor would go away and not require more surgery as we prepared for Dallin's arrival to our family.

The rest of the summer consisted of trips to the "big pool" (Seven Peaks Waterpark), weekly movie mornings at the Cinemark theaters, and time spent with the family. We went on the little rides at a small amusement park, dressed up like cows for some free Chick-fil-A, and enjoyed playing with friends. It was nice to get back to normal and enjoy our little family of three.

The day that Dallin was set to be born, we dropped Holland off at her friend Alice's house until my parents could come pick her up. Dallin was born at American Fork Hospital and that evening Holland was able to come by and finally meet her little brother. She got to hold him and also see Mommy take her turn staying in the hospital. It was cute to watch her study his face and try to figure out this new little boy.

The Third Surgery

A few months later, Holland had another MRI to check on the status of the tumor. Many people had been earnestly praying throughout the summer that the tumor would shrink and go away on its own. Unfortunately, this was not the case. We found out that the tumor was unchanged and would require another surgery to have it removed. Heartbroken, we scheduled the surgery for a few weeks later.

Since she was not symptomatic (as she had been before her first surgery), we took the next couple of weeks to do fun things that she wanted to do. We went to a friend's birthday party where she got to bounce in a fun house, get her face painted (she wanted a yellow angry bird, but the girl didn't know how to paint that so she settled for a yellow spider), and pet some animals, like a turtle and a chinchilla. We also went to Farm Country at Thanksgiving Point in Lehi, Utah, where she got to pet some more animals, like cows, horses, and llamas, and she got to go on her first pony ride! I took Holland to the open football practice for BYU (and bought her popcorn and ice cream to keep her entertained). Since Dallin was only about two weeks old, we skipped the camping part of the ward campout and instead, we made s'mores on our gas grill, and Holland and I spent the night in the tent in the backyard. She definitely had a hard time falling asleep and woke up early, but she had fun with all of the glow sticks. The next morning we drove up Spanish Fork Canyon to join the rest of the ward for breakfast. Holland had fun exploring around the lake and throwing rocks in it.

On the morning of Holland's third brain surgery, we had to check in at 9:15 a.m. Aleta's mom came down from Washington to help with Dallin since he was not allowed in the PICU, allowing Aleta to spend more time with Holland. It was almost weird to check in for surgery because, although Holland had already had two surgeries, this route of prepping for the surgery was different than the rushed emergency surgeries we had experienced before.

We checked in, they took her vitals, and we got her the "cool jammies" (the hospital gown). We then waited in the pre-op waiting room where Holland played with some toys while we waited to talk to Dr. Burkes and the anesthesiologist. Holland was so good—she was happy (even though she was fasting) and had fun playing with the doctor kit and giving everyone shots. We were relieved to see her so happy even though she was back at the hospital. The anesthesiologist was amazing with her. After he talked to us, he said, "Okay, Holland, do you want a ride in my arms or do you want to walk?" She chose to walk, so he took her by the hand and showed her exactly where we were going: past the dog poster, following the hot air balloon tiles on the floor, pointing out all the little things to look for. We got to the surgery room's double doors and he said, "Okay, give Mom and Dad a kiss!" We hugged her and she turned around and started skipping down the hall with the doctor. It was a funny sight to see this little three-year-old next to a tall (probably 6'5") doctor. At one point she started going in the wrong room but quickly came back

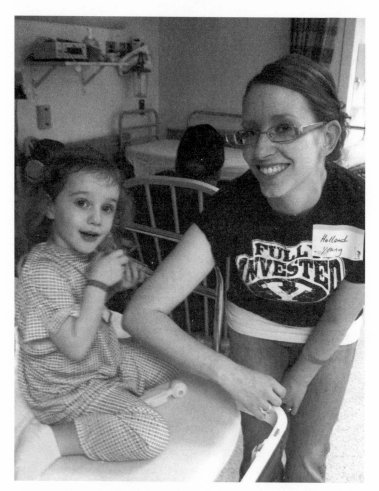

out and continued skipping off to surgery. We went to our usual place in the surgery waiting room. This surgery was shorter, only three and a half or four hours. At the end, Dr. Burkes came in and told us that it went well and he was able to get it out and that Holland did well during the procedure.

The Fourth Surgery

Holland had a follow-up MRI the next morning to make sure everything looked good. To our disbelief, the tumor was still there! And unchanged! We were baffled—how did this happen?

What did he take out instead? And *why?* She had already been through so much and it was devastating that we were now facing yet another surgery! Dr. Burkes, though usually quite confident in his own abilities, was certainly humbled when he talked to us. He said he was very disappointed—he believed what he took out was tumor. He seemed to take the news as hard—if not harder— than we did. It looked like tumor material, it was where the tumor should have been, and the pathology had confirmed that it was indeed the tumor. Unfortunately, it was not the tumor, but essentially scar tissue. He said they were duped by the pathology. He also told us if we wanted to go with a different doctor, that he would understand. "If I were in your position," he said, "I would be disgusted with myself as a doctor." We both felt, however, that we should not go with a different doctor. After all, Dr. Burkes had seen the inside of her brain three times now, which was certainly a benefit that another doctor would not have.

Going forward, he pulled out all the stops, giving us options we didn't know were possible. For the next surgery, we planned to do a pre-op MRI to computer map the location of the tumor, do the surgery with a robotic scope, and immediately do a post-op MRI to confirm. We also asked that a second doctor be asked to assist in the surgery. We had come this far with Dr. Burkes and didn't want to start all over with another surgeon now, but another set of trained eyes couldn't hurt.

As we sent her away to surgery for the fourth time in three months, we felt a bit nervous. I wished I could have gone to the temple, but I knew that I needed to be there for her when she woke up. So I called my dad and then Aleta's dad, requesting that they both go to the temple while Holland was in surgery. Meanwhile, we returned to our familiar home in the surgery waiting room.

As Holland had an MRI before surgery this time, we were away from her much longer, nearly all day. Dr. Burkes came back and said that they did the initial frozen biopsy and he and Dr. Carter (the assisting doctor) had both triple checked it. They were very confident that they had gotten it all and the mapped out

scans showed that they had
worked in the right place.
We knew this time that it
was all gone. Immediately
after the surgery Holland
went in for her post-op
MRI, and then we were
finally able to be with her in
the PICU.

As she started recover-
ing from what appeared to
be her final surgery, one of
the residents came in with
the results of the scan. And
finally we had the good
news that they had successfully removed the entire

tumor. The next few days were much smoother, since we were
filled with the optimism that we might finally be done. We had
many family members and friends stop by to visit, and we had
much happier interactions with the doctors. Holland enjoyed
playing in the playrooms and seeing her favorite sights of the
hospital before we headed home from the hospital for what felt
like the last time.

Trying to Get Back to Normal

We returned home, I returned to work, and our life started to
return to some sense of normalcy. My sister Jamie had set up a
donation site, and as a result, we were very thankful to receive
about three thousand dollars in donations, which helped with the
rising medical costs.

Over the summer I had started attending the temple more
regularly to better understand the Lord's will for Holland. One
day before work, I attended the temple and received the distinct
revelation that we had endured this trial well but that it was not

over. The Lord also said that we should not fear, for great blessings were in store. I never would have dreamed the shape those blessings would take.

Holland had a follow-up appointment with Dr. Burkes in October. Everything checked out: her scar was healing well and she was feeling good. Dr. Burkes seemed to think everything was fine. He recommended that we have a follow-up MRI in February, but he seemed optimistic that she would have no new growth. None of us would have expected that at that very moment a new tumor and cyst had already begun to form.

The rest of the fall went as expected for a three-year-old girl. We enjoyed dressing as *Monsters, Inc.* characters for Halloween and going to the movies together. She also enjoyed playing in the fall leaves and the early snow.

5

Sick Again

At the beginning of December, Holland started randomly asking me for priesthood blessings. I explained to her that they are very special and only for when we aren't feeling well. She told me that her head hurt and so I did give her a blessing. One morning before I left for work, Holland asked for a blessing because her head hurt again. In this blessing the Lord said, "This pain is not a result of your tumor returning and in the coming days the pain will subside." So I went to work feeling good that she would get better.

That Saturday night, she had a rough night sleeping, and when she woke up she started throwing up again. The whole thing felt too familiar, so we called the on-call neurosurgeon at Primary's and decided to check into the ER. A CT scan revealed some growth but it was unclear what the growth was, so we had an MRI as well. The results showed that a small amount of tumor about the size of a quarter had returned, and that a cyst the size of an orange had formed and begun to put pressure on her ventricles again. So we decided to stay in the hospital overnight and wait to talk to Dr. Burkes the next morning.

The next day, after returning from attending one of my favorite wards there at the hospital, Dr. Burkes came to the hospital just to meet with us. It was weird to see him in more casual clothes. He said he had never seen something like this where a JPA grew back this quickly and this aggressively. He also pointed out that there was a small bit of growth about the size of a pencil tip that was away from the original tumor site, which was very concerning. He recommended that Holland once again go into surgery, so we scheduled her fifth surgery for the following afternoon.

The Blessing of the Lord's Servants

The next day, before the surgery, we were blessed to have two members of the Quorum of the Seventy visit and give Holland, Aleta, and myself priesthood blessings. Our good friend Bridget Smith had called the personal secretary to President Thomas S. Monson, who then called President Monson. As members of the Quorum of the Twelve don't often make house calls, he agreed to send two members of the Quorum of the Seventy. After phone tag and commuting through a snowstorm, they showed up at about noon, an hour before Holland's surgery.

As it so happens, I had met one of them on my mission, when he was an Area Seventy over Idaho, and he was very excited when I reminded him of this. His presence was a tender mercy to me. Meanwhile, Holland was not feeling great and had been very agitated most of that day. She calmed down for the blessing though. I do not remember all the words of the blessing, but I remember he stated that the blessing was under the direction of President Monson. He asked a blessing that the doctors would be guided and led by the Spirit during the surgery. The blessing said that tumors and cancers would continue to plague her body, but she would be happy and healthy. There was also a blessing that she would live to be an adult and a mother and have a family of her own.

The elders then assisted me in giving Aleta a blessing, and then gave me a blessing. Once again, I do not remember all the words that were said but I know that we were both given strength to lead our family and be an example to others. After the General Authorities left, Aleta and I were left to think about what was said. We both knew that things were going to get worse before they got better. We felt that Holland would need to have chemotherapy but that things would work out. Although we were a little fearful at the prospect of chemo, we felt an overall peace that we were in the Lord's hands.

The Fifth Surgery

A few hours later, after her pre-surgery MRI, we watched the door close to the operating area for the fifth time in six months. But this time there was a peace we hadn't felt before that we were going to be okay even though we were in for a ride. In the waiting room, Aleta, my parents, and I played with Dallin. Watching this happy boy, it was hard to believe that his sister was down the hall being cut open for brain surgery. Even though there was a feeling of peace and happiness, my body was beginning to wear down. While waiting, I became sick and threw up in the waiting room bathroom.

After several hours, Dr. Burkes informed us that they had been extra aggressive in making sure they removed everything that needed to come out, in hopes of preventing another surgery. They removed everything that was in question: the cyst, the cyst wall, the tumor, the smaller tumor, and more scar tissue. He said that they had triple checked the frozen biopsy to confirm that this was indeed the correct tumor. It did appear to be a new kind of tumor, but we wouldn't know for sure until the pathology returned in a week or so. He was once again optimistic that he had gotten it all out. The plan was to leave her intubated overnight so that they could do the follow-up MRI in the morning without requiring her to recover from sedation just to be put under again.

After the surgery, they had tied down her arms again because even though she was still under, she had tried to remove the breathing tube. Throughout the night, Holland was fully sedated with the most powerful drugs, but she still managed to wake up five times, trying to rip out her breathing tube each time, fighting off as many as eight adults.

6

My Own Personal Miracle

We thought we'd learned what the Lord needed us to learn, so the recurrence of the tumor had been really hard for Aleta and me to take. We felt like we had made it through the fire with our faith intact. We had learned so many lessons about faith, priesthood, the temple, the Spirit, the will of the Lord, love, and family—lessons that we couldn't have learned any other way. But now those bitter feelings of doubt began to creep in again. Saturday night, the first night back in the hospital, I had called my dad to tell him the news. In despair I told him, "Dad, it feels like there isn't anything I can do."

He replied, "Well, son, you can always pray."

I laughed and sneered at him, saying, "What good has that done me? If it was as simple as saying a prayer, don't you think it would be over?" I had prayed, fasted, given priesthood blessings, received priesthood blessings, and our family and friends had done the same, and now here we were, back at square one.

Since Holland was intubated all of Monday night, I took the opportunity to sleep on a real bed in a parent room in the PICU. This, however, was one of my least restful nights at the hospital. The following is a letter I wrote to sum up the events of the night to the two members of the Seventy that had visited with us:

37

Meant for Heaven

Brethren,

I write this email to you in the middle of the night, from my bed in the parents' unit of the pediatric intensive care unit, to tell you an experience that has truly humbled me to the core. After you left our room yesterday, my wife and I discussed the peace that we felt as a result of the blessing from the Lord that you Brethren were the conduits of. My wife and I also shared the collective feeling that our daughter's one benign tumor was now malignant. Although we were assured through the blessing that Holland would indeed live through this ordeal, we also felt the ominous feeling that things would get worse before they got better. After the surgery her doctor indeed confirmed that the tumor had changed to a more aggressive tumor. The exact nature of this tumor and the fact that it could be cancerous will not be known until a complete pathology is done in the next few days. We were both at peace with this knowledge, as the Lord had already revealed this to us through the blessing.

But my weak physical body became overwhelmed with the stress. Shortly after the doctor left, I went to the bathroom and threw up. My stomach was overcome by the stress of the moment. As I returned to her room in the PICU and saw my daughter's near lifeless body . . . my own body continued to feel weak. I tried to eat but my body began to chill and I felt sick. I went to bed but my stomach turned and my mind raced, thinking of all the possible trials and hardships the future holds for our young family. About an hour ago I left my bed and went to the bathroom sick again, and, after returning to my bed, I was overcome by the feeling to once again turn to the Lord in prayer. . . . As I knelt, tears filled my eyes as I asked the Lord take away this sickness from me so that I could be strong enough to serve my family. I felt the presence of other beings and the impression of hands on my head. The words of the blessing returned to my mind and peace returned and then the words of the temple blessings entered my mind. I felt the Lord immediately bless each part of my body as He had once blessed me within the temple. The pain in my stomach began to decrease and my mind began to settle down.

Chapter 6

I then felt prompted to look up some conference talks on my phone to further calm my mind. I first searched for talks about the Atonement and came across a talk by one of you about the life of your brother. The words of the Spirit told me that just as Christ had overcome sin to allow us to repent, He also overcame death to allow us to be made whole physically. And although the results of sin have eternal consequences, the results of physical limitation and illness are only temporary. After listening to this talk, my mind was clear and I remembered the experiences from this past general conference, when I was particularly touched by a talk from a member of the Quorum of the Seventy. I found this talk and pressed play. Tears filled my eyes and the love of the Lord filled my heart as I saw the face and then the name of [the other elder]. I realized the tender mercies of the Lord: He had not only sent me two of his servants to minister to me, but He had sent the very man who had brought me to tears this last October. Tears began to stream down my face as I listened to your words as you recounted the feelings of, "Why me?" at the loss of your young son. These were the same feelings of bitterness toward the Lord that I had once felt at finding out that Holland had a brain tumor. I was truly humbled by the fact that through you two, His servants, the Lord had remembered me and given me the counsel I needed in my moment of despair. My illness is now gone, and as I conclude my words here my mind is now clear and able to rest with what nighttime I have left. I thank you, Brethren, for your ability and worthiness to answer the call to be special witnesses of Christ.

You have indeed magnified that call, and you ministered to my family and me physically today and then again to me tonight in spirit through your inspired conference addresses. I hope at this late hour I was able to clearly express the impact that you both have had on me. I now know with greater resolve that the Lord is ever mindful of me and will never leave me in my time of need. His words and yours will carry me through this trial in my life. Thank you both so very much.

Love,
Your brother in the gospel,
Bryan Young

The next morning Aleta arrived in time to watch over Holland as she went through yet another MRI. The events of the night before had been great to lift my spirit and had given me a sense of the Lord's presence in my life, but I needed to talk with Him personally in His house, away from all the distractions of the moment. So I decided to take the TRAX (Salt Lake Valley's light rail system) to the Salt Lake Temple. The sessions at this temple take a little bit longer than they do at other temples, but I appreciated the extra time there. I felt peace as I arrived in the celestial room, but I had come to talk with the Lord, not just to enjoy the atmosphere. I sat down, bowed my head, and asked the Lord, "Why are we going through this again? Haven't we learned enough lessons? Why haven't You heard our prayers? I thought there were great blessings coming our way. This doesn't feel like a blessing at all. Thank You for sending me Your servants and being mindful, but I have felt very alone throughout this process. Why did You spare her life just to have us go through this again?"

At this point, tears filled my eyes and I was overwhelmed emotionally. Then the soft peace and clarity of the Lord's voice in my mind came through the frustration and anger. "My son, I have not left you. I am with you always and I will continue to be with you throughout this trial. She will survive this but your trials are not over. You still have major blessings in store as well. Know this: if not for your faith and prayers and the faith and prayers of your family and friends, she would have died last June. Trust in me and things will work out according to My will. Continue to trust in Me even as things get worse, and you and your family will make it through this."

As I prepared to leave the temple, I sat in the changing stall and was overcome with emotion. Tears filled my eyes, not because of the upcoming challenges that the Lord had just told me about, but due to the love I was shown. I was overcome with the presence of the Lord in my life. I knew He was with us then, that He had been the whole time, and that He would continue to bless and comfort us going forward. As I rode the TRAX back to the hospital, I knew that regardless of the results of Holland's

MRI, everything would be okay. I had such peace because the Lord was with us.

Good News

When I got back, Holland was out of the MRI and starting to wake up again. Her voice was raspy, but she was speaking. Her hands were shaky, but she was moving. Our prayers had once again been answered, as it appeared that she would still be able to walk and talk, which was a risk with every brain surgery. The doctors assured us that the quiet raspy voice was a typical result of the twenty-four-hour breathing tube she'd had in.

Not long after she woke up, the doctors returned with the MRI images. The tumor was completely gone. They had been extra aggressive, trying to remove all that they could so as to avoid another surgery, and they had been successful. I teased Dr. Burkes, telling him, "Now that you've gotten it all out in one surgery, we don't know what to do—we're so used to it taking two!" He seemed a little hurt by that, but the nurses all laughed and said he needed to hear that to humble him. Before we left, I did apologize and thank him profusely for saving our daughter's life again.

We again began the now familiar process of recovery. The next few days were filled with great support from family and friends, both in visits to the hospital and Facebook messages of support. Holland began to regain her strength and personality. She was always grumpy after her surgeries—and justifiably so— but she again started to find joy in her shows and playing with toys and games.

Three days after her surgery, we were in the neuro trauma unit (NTU) and they gave us the option to go home or stay another day. She was still grumpy but able to move around and do most things on her own. They trusted us to take care of her at home just as well as they would at the hospital, so after some debate we decided to go home. We packed everything up, waited for Holland to wake up, and drove home that evening through snowy roads, glad to be home in our own beds.

7

Christmas with Cancer

Over the next several days we tried to get back to normal life. I went back to work, and that weekend we went to church as planned. Holland was gaining back her energy and personality. She was even able to play in the snow and build a snow fort less than a week after her surgery.

A week before Christmas, we went to Dr. Ryan to have the stitches removed. He was concerned about the swelling at her incision site and recommended that we call Dr. Burkes and have him check it out. When we called, they had just received her pathology results, so we returned to the hospital to discuss the results. Dr. Burkes informed us that the tumor had indeed mutated into a pilomyxoid astrocytoma (PMA), a grade 2 tumor that was more aggressive. Inspecting Holland's swelling, he said her dura lining (the membrane that holds in the CSF surrounding the brain) had most likely burst and CSF had started to leak, but he was not too concerned. He told us that the following week, the tumor board would meet and decide what course of treatment to take going forward. The tumor board was a group of experts and doctors—neurologists, oncologists, surgeons, and other specialists—who reviewed and discussed medical conditions and treatment options. He said that most likely since the tumor had mutated so quickly and was behaving so aggressively we would need to do chemotherapy.

Dr. Burkes did, however, give us the clearance to go forward with our holiday plans to drive down to Las Vegas. When we arrived, Holland was doing well. She was loving playtime and slumber parties with her cousins.

However, on Christmas Eve, she started to get sick. She had no energy and a high fever, and her scar site was even more swollen than before. It appeared that she was having some complications. That night, two of Holland's uncles and two of her cousins gave her a blessing. Despite this, she was not able to participate in any of the fun Christmas Eve festivities. She stayed at her cousins' house with Aleta that night, and later we opened one of her presents. Holland barely had the strength to open it, let alone show any excitement.

That night was filled with fever and tears, since she was not able to get the rest she desperately needed. Christmas morning found her lacking energy and quietly laying down as everyone else excitedly opened presents. The occasional gift would elicit some interest from her but mostly she was too sick to enjoy it. Christmas night, as she awoke in tears, my brother-in-law and I were prompted to give her a blessing in which Heavenly Father said that on this night of celebrating Christ's birth, Christ Himself would be permitted to personally administer to her throughout the night. Christ was not only aware of her pain and struggles, but He was actually with her as He had been before. That night she had some ups and downs, but mostly peace.

On Christmas day Holland was featured on the Primary Children's blog in an article titled "12 Miracles of Christmas."[1] We had been interviewed by a staff member and told that they would post our story on their blog. We were a little surprised that she was the final story featured though. That day, our donation website received a donation that put us above our six thousand dollar goal. It was so humbling to be the recipient of these blessings.

Chapter 7

Although we enjoyed being in Las Vegas with family, Holland was experiencing more downs than ups, so we went back home a few days after Christmas. As an answer to our prayers, her fever had gone down and she was relatively happy on the drive back. The next night, however, her fever had returned. The doctors at Primary Children's had told us that if her fever returned, we should take her to the emergency room, so the next morning she and I went to the ER. The doctors there conferred with her doctors at Primary's and concluded that the fever was the result of a cold on top of her recovery from the surgery. So they sent us home with some antibiotics.

Entering the World of Oncology

Just after New Year's Day, we went in to meet with Dr. Shephard, Holland's oncologist. She walked us through the chemo schedule: After a surgery to get a port inserted, Holland would have weekly treatments of vincristine for a month. After that she would start monthly treatments for twelve months with carboplatin added to the vincristine. These words and the whole process of chemo were a bit overwhelming but we took it all in stride. Dr. Shephard was concerned with the swelling at Holland's scar site. She called Dr. Burkes's office and they made an appointment for us to meet with him the next day.

The next day brought another visit to Primary Children's Hospital, where Dr. Burkes inspected the swelling and was more concerned than he had been before Christmas. He said that there was a chance that it could be an infection or a more serious condition known as hydrocephalus, which is an increased amount of CSF that causes pressure on the brain. He said they would need to do a spinal tap to run tests on her CSF for infections. So the next day brought our third visit to Primary's in as many days.

That morning we discovered a new wing of the hospital, same-day surgery. Since this area is for quick surgeries that don't require overnight stays, there were only two surgery prep rooms. We waited while Holland watched movies on the Holland Movie

Channel and played with the child play specialist, which is a specialist who is employed to play with sick kids to help take their minds off what they're going through. Soon Dr. Burkes and some of his residents came in to take Holland into the main surgery room, where she was put under with gas for the first time. She chose the root beer–flavored gas. Aleta took Dallin out to the cafeteria while I waited just over a half an hour for Holland's spinal tap.

When Holland woke up from the anesthesia, she was grumpier than normal, crying and yelling even though they had snacks and soda for her. They offered her a stuffed dog for being so brave, but she said very curtly, "I don't want it!"

I looked at the recovery nurse apologetically and told her, "Just put it with our stuff; I'm sure she will want it later." When Aleta and Dallin came in, we were told we could go home. I grabbed our stuff and the dog, and Holland, still groggy from the anesthesia, protested that we were taking the dog.

The next morning, when Holland woke up, she was her normal happy self, especially because the spinal tap had reduced the swelling at her scar site. She was happy until she found the dog. "I told you to leave it at the hospital!" she exclaimed angrily.

The results of the spinal tap showed that she didn't have an infection but due to the many surgeries, she had too much blood and CSF in her brain and had developed hydrocephalus. The pressure on her brain was so high they said that when they put the tap in, CSF shot across the room. She had an estimated brain pressure of 30 PSI—though the average human brain is 10–15 PSI. Because of the hydrocephalus, Holland needed to have an internal shunt implanted to drain the excess CSF from her ventricles down a tube behind her ear and into her stomach, where her body would dispose of it as normal. The doctors decided that, during the surgery to install the shunt, they would put in the port for her chemo treatments as well.

When we went home that night, I began to get sick as well and couldn't keep anything down. I tried to sleep but was so restless that I went downstairs to lay on the couch so as not to wake up Aleta. After several more trips to the bathroom, I attempted to stand up, but I was too weak and I collapsed on the floor. I called out to Aleta, who eventually came downstairs and helped me back onto the couch. I was shaking and had a very high fever. My body was starting to shut down from all the stress. We thought maybe we should go to the ER but decided to first call someone for a priesthood blessing. The only problem was that it was 3:00 a.m. We called our home teacher, my fellow members of the elders quorum presidency, the bishopric, and old friends. No one picked up. After many tries, our former neighbor and good friend picked up and agreed to come over and give me a blessing.

The blessing gave me just what I needed, and we did not need to go to the ER. I was promised that I would be able to continue to help Holland with her surgeries and be a strength for my family. After the blessing, I immediately started to improve, though I laid low that weekend, recuperating so that I could be strong enough to stay at the hospital with Holland for her surgery on Monday.

Surgery Number Six

Holland's sixth brain surgery in as many months was not nearly as invasive as the others had been. Since this surgery involved two different procedures, there were two different surgeons present. Dr. Burkes would put in the shunt and Dr. Barnhart would put in the chemo port (also known as a PICC line or direct line). Holland was such a pro at the surgery prep at this point; she knew what toys she wanted to play with in the waiting room and was laughing and smiling as the anesthesiologist took her into the operating room in a wagon. Part of me was happy that she was having fun at the hospital but another part of me found it hard to see her so used to the idea of going into surgery.

Aleta and I had also grown accustomed to the surgery waiting room and the nurses there knew us by name. We watched the mixed emotions of the other parents with a sense of wisdom and experience that we didn't have before. Both Dr. Burkes and

Dr. Barnhart came to tell us about the surgery progress and that all had gone well. This surgery took only a couple of hours and seemed to fly right by. And since this surgery wasn't as intensive, Holland didn't need to go to the PICU afterward for recovery, so we met her in the surgery recovery room, which we had never been in before, and, after she was stable enough, we went to the NTU floor.

Holland was really uncomfortable and had a hard time straightening out her neck, which made it hard for her to sleep and relax. She did have a great time watching her favorite movies and going to the playroom though. And after a couple of days, Holland was cleared to go home. Two days later, there was a large snowstorm, and Holland and I went outside to build a snow fort. It was amazing to me that this little girl could be playing in the snow and having so much fun just days after her sixth brain surgery. Kids really are incredibly resilient.

That same day, my grandmother, Grandma Young, passed away. While Holland at three years old was fighting so hard to stay alive, my grandma—at ninety-eight years old—was so tired and ready to be reunited with her husband after an eighteen-year absence. A week later, Holland was cleared to go on a short road trip up to Idaho Falls for Grandma's funeral. This was not only a fun time for Holland to spend with cousins and other family, but it also gave us the opportunity to explain to Holland what death really meant. This was an important lesson to learn as her treatments got harder, so she could understand the reason for undergoing chemo.

The First of Many Chemo Appointments

Before our trip up to Idaho for my grandma's funeral, we had Holland's first chemo appointment. When we left for the hospital that morning, we discovered a present on our front doorstep: two stockings filled with candy and toys, including two stuffed snowmen that Holland happily played with during the drive to the hospital. We still don't know who left that gift for Holland or if they knew that it was Holland's first chemo appointment, but to us it was a tender mercy from the Lord.

The average chemo appointment involved a lot. We had to numb her port before leaving the house. We then packed up her dolls from the movie *Brave* to remind Holland to be brave, then we drove to the hospital. When we arrived, we would check in and wait in the front room. My parents usually came to stay with Dallin, since he wasn't allowed into any of the back rooms where the patients were. Once we got called back, Holland had her height, weight, and blood pressure measured. Next we went back to a room where Holland got to play with the oncology child life specialist, Raquel. Holland always liked the toys and games that Raquel would bring in. Then Holland's nurse, Jennifer, would come in to access her port—which Holland hated—and draw her blood to check her counts before treatments could begin. Sometimes the oncology social worker, Leah, would come in to get an idea of how our family was doing and to see if we needed help or support. Then Dr. Shephard would come in and give us the count information, check Holland's general health, and answer any questions we had. Then we would go back to the "blue room," as the staff called it, and start Holland's chemo treatments while she watched cartoons, did arts and crafts, played with toys, and ate popsicles. Afterward, we de-accessed her port, which was sometimes harder than accessing it. Finally, we checked out and scheduled our return appointment. And if Holland had been good, we would stop at the toy store or 7-Eleven for treats and prizes on the way home.

The next several weeks and months were filled with this chemo routine. Like a roller coaster, this routine had its ups and downs, but we learned to enjoy the ride. It was sometimes hard to sit and watch cartoons while your child was literally being pumped full of poisons, but we not only trusted the doctors and nurses, but we felt that this was right by the Lord and the correct course to take. With all the surgeries and doctor's appointments, I missed a lot of work, and, in February, that caught up with me. There was some difficulty in filing the forms to request time off and accounting for the time I had missed, but things eventually worked out and I was able to get the days off without further problems with my employer. This negative interaction taught me how much more important my family, and especially this little girl, was to me than anything else in my life. I was willing to lose my job if it came to it so that I could do what was best for her and help her in any way I could. I could make a living in any number of ways, but I only had one Holland—and I was going to do all I could not to lose her.

Notes

1. "12 Days of Miracles: Day 12 Holland's Miracle: How a Cyst Turned into a Miracle," *Primary Children's Hospital* (blog), December 25, 2012, www.primarychildrenshospitalblog.org/?s=2012.

8

The Ministering of Angels

After a month or so of chemo, Holland's immune system was significantly weaker, and she started to get sick. In early February, she couldn't sleep due to an ear infection and cold. She was up all night, complaining of fever and pain. I had given her a blessing before she went to bed, as I often had to do to help her sleep. Just after midnight I went in to give her a second priesthood blessing, in which the Lord promised that angels would administer to her throughout the night. I sat with her after the blessing was over and continued to pray because she was still crying out in pain.

I started to pray specifically that the blessing would be fulfilled and she could receive the help of angels to finally get the rest she needed for just this night. She calmed down for a bit and the Lord told me to put my hand on her head. When I did, I could feel another hand on her head, but I could not see anything. I could sense the presence of many beings in the room, though it appeared empty except for Holland and myself. I prayed to see more clearly what was happening around me. The Lord opened my spiritual eyes to see what and who were around me. Though I could not physically describe what I experienced, I knew that they were there. If you walked into a pitch-black room, you wouldn't be able to see who was in the room, but you would definitely be able to tell or feel if other people were there. Similarly, I could feel the presence of other people in the room.

The Lord told me that there were three angels ministering to Holland: David, Samuel, and Betsie (Bertha). He also told me that the spirits of my family members were present to watch over and comfort our family: my paternal grandparents and Aleta's brother and maternal grandfather. It is important to note that I had never met Aleta's brother or grandfather in this life—in fact, I didn't even know Aleta's grandfather was named John. He was not a member of the Church, but I was told that he had accepted the gospel in the spirit world and was grateful for the temple work that had been done in his name years before.

Once again I could not see them, but I could spiritually feel that there were three spirits around Holland and at least four standing around the foot of her bed. Holland had fallen peacefully to sleep after hours of pain and agony. I went back to my room, lay in my bed, and typed the following passage into my phone:

> The Lord had authorized me to call upon these angels and spirits to bring peace to Holland in her time of need. It is not His will that this trial be taken from her at this time, but He does desire that her pain and sickness be healed and that she find rest. I felt them, I heard them, and the Lord showed my spirit where they were. I have witnessed a miracle—I have witnessed this night the hand of the Lord intervening directly in the lives of His children. I cannot deny these experiences and the peace that I have felt.

I then drifted off to sleep. The next morning I handed Aleta my phone so she could read what had happened the night before while she was asleep. I then detailed to her the entire account as I remembered it. A few minutes later Holland awoke and came in our room. She had peacefully slept the rest of the night without interruption. I asked her, "How did you sleep, Holland?"

She replied, "I slept good. The angels helped me." Aleta and I both looked at each other, stunned, since she had never mentioned anything like this before. We asked her if she could see them, and she said, "I could see their hands. They had white hands and gave me a special prayer like Daddy."

"How many were there?" we asked.

She thought for a second and began to count out loud and she pointed around the room, "Ummm, there was 1 . . . 2 . . . 3 . . . 4 . . . 5." It was like she was trying to recall exactly where she had seen them. She then climbed into bed with us as if it were a typical Sunday morning.

Although her exact count of spirits was somewhat different than mine, I knew at this moment that this event had truly occurred. It had been confirmed by the humble innocent voice of my suffering three-year-old daughter. I had not coached her or prompted her to say that. She knew just as I did that angels had surrounded us the night before. And in her own way, she knew as I knew that the Lord was mindful of our family and would never leave us to suffer alone. Although she was not miraculously cured from cancer that night, a miracle occurred just the same: the Lord intervened in our lives to give one of His many suffering children a small respite from the pain. This was not the only such event to occur in my life, but it will always be one of the most sacred encounters because I experienced it with Holland.

Fund-Raisers

The cost of Holland's medical bills were starting to add up. In less than a year, our costs were already over ten thousand dollars. As a young educator, that was about a fourth of my yearly salary. Fortunately, we had been saving up to buy a house so we had more than usual in our savings account. Aleta and I had agreed that if we put off buying a house, we would have enough money to pay for all Holland's medical bills. So financially we were fine—not great, but not struggling by any means.

But we found that when you are in helpless situations, like having a child with cancer, people want to help but don't know how. My sister set up a giveforward.com account for us, and we opened up a donation account at Wells Fargo for people to contribute to. Also, during Christmastime many people had given us money and extra gifts for the kids. These kind monetary donations provided for many of our medical expenses, bringing in several thousand dollars. While it can be hard to be the recipient of other people's sacrifices and charity, I had learned years before, on my mission, that accepting help from other people is almost more about letting them grow from the sacrifice and service than it is about the gain that you receive as the person in need.

Even though we had received much and were financially able to pay all our bills, many people were looking for ways they could help our family. Two of our good friends separately contacted us about doing fund-raisers. One of my friends, Nancy, from grad school, approached me around Christmastime about doing a 5K for Holland. She was working at Spanish Fork High School with the Latinos in Action program, and the previous year they had done a 5K for a family of a little boy with leukemia as a class service project. Our other friend who contacted us was our good friend Katie, who wanted to hold a charity Zumbathon for Holland. She was a Zumba instructor and volunteered to organize the event.

Since 5Ks are best held in warm weather, the Zumbathon was held first, in late February at the gym at the Vivint complex in the Riverwoods business park. Katie recruited the Kaufusi family to help out as well. The Kaufusi's daughter, Alexis, was a former BYU basketball player and a cancer survivor who had just recently battled non-Hodgkin's lymphoma.

Alexis had a blog to keep people updated on her treatment, and she wanted to meet and interview us so she could post our story and advertise for the Zumbathon on her blog. Here are some excerpts from that post:

> Yesterday my mother, Michelle, texted me, telling me she had an idea and needed my opinion. Naturally I called her, wondering what she would possibly want my opinion about, and she said that there was a little girl who was three. Her name

Chapter 8

was Holland. She's from Provo and from an avid BYU family, and she had multiple brain tumors. Immediately I felt as if my heart weighed twenty pounds as it sunk into my chest. I then told Chelle we needed to do what we could to help this little girl and her family out, just like all of you helped me out.

* * Fast-forward twenty-four hours * *

As we approached the home where Holland Young lives, I couldn't help but be so nervous. Out front was a metal yard decoration sporting the BYU logo, but then my attention was directed to the squealing giggles of a little girl as the front door opened. As we walked in we were greeted by Holland's mother, Aleta, and her six-month-old brother, Dallin. We were then introduced to Bryan, Holland's father, then to a small girl on the couch. To be honest, my first impression was, *Wow, she's tiny.* There she was, not even weighing fifty pounds—little Holland, curled up on the couch playing a game on an iPad. . . . She's small, pretty pale, but I could just sense the fire that was burning within her. . . .

Amidst all this chaos and catastrophe though, never in a million years would I have guessed that Holland would have been through so much suffering. Watching her today she had energy. She was all over the room, playing games on the iPad. She was oozing with emotion as she would win and lose. You couldn't miss the smile and excitement when she downloaded a new game. Bryan also told me she had a nice follow-through and jump shot as well. Just being in the presence of this little warrior, I felt inspired. I fed off her strength and in this young girl I couldn't help but see myself. She was sassy, stubborn, and you could tell she knew she wasn't going to lose this fight.[1]

The day of the Zumbathon, Holland was really excited. She wore some of my sweatbands and her sweatpants. It started snowing on our way there and didn't let up all day. When we arrived, Holland and I went up on stage with Katie. While Katie was leading the dancing, Holland and I did our own dancing, which consisted of running around and me spinning her in circles. Many friends from our current and old ward came out, including a lot of my family and a few old friends. Alexis's brother who played football for BYU also came to support us with a few other players. We also met many strangers who were really just there because they loved Zumba but were willing to reach out and help our family. Holland had fun running around with the kids and dancing to her own moves. It was truly humbling to be the recipient of that much kindness and generosity.

After the Zumbathon, life went back to normal (or at least our new normal) for another couple of months. Holland continued to have monthly chemo treatments, and for the most part, she was handling them very well and getting used to the oncology rooms and staff at Primary's. It was during this time that I began to reflect on the roller-coaster ride that we had been on for the last eight or nine months. This reflection helped me realize how fortunate we were to have this little girl in our life and how much of a miracle each moment of her life was.

Getting ready for the 5K in April, we did a couple of interviews with local newspapers: the *Daily Herald* in Provo and the BYU newspaper, *The Daily Universe*. (Those articles are available at the end of this book in Appendix D and Appendix E, respectively.)

A few days before the race, Holland, Aleta, and Dallin went to Spanish Fork High School to meet the class of kids who were putting on the race for her. We had filmed some promos for the race that they played on the video morning announcements, so when Holland showed up at the school everyone knew who she was. Aleta said it was like being a celebrity with everyone talking to her and looking at her. The kids from Latinos in Action loved working with Holland, and they were all really sweet to her.

When the day of the race arrived, it was really cold and windy. Holland was able to hold the megaphone and count down to the start of the race. Though she was a little shy at first, she stepped right up to it when her time came. I was planning to run the race, and I had told Holland that she could just take the shortcut and meet everyone at the finish line. But when the race started, she insisted on going with me. So we ran just a couple of blocks while I tried to convince her to go back. Then she tripped

Chapter 8

and skinned her knee and started to cry, so we went to the finish line, where we got to hang out with Cosmo, Nancy, and a bunch of friends and family.

Although Holland didn't run the race, she was still full of energy and was running and jumping around. We cheered for the runners as they started to come in to the stadium where the race ended. As people came running in, it was again truly humbling to see all of these people—some from many different times in our lives, and many we hardly knew—all there to support this little girl. As each person came up to meet the little girl of the hour and take pictures, Holland just kept innocently and obliviously playing with her friends. Through all of this I continued to be amazed at how good people are.

The blessings of these fund-raisers were so much more than money. It was a chance to touch lives, to inspire hope, to lift up

57

the broken hearts, and to unite people in a good cause. Holland and our little family were not the only recipients. The blessings flowed right back to each volunteer and participant who took time from their own lives to care about ours. The Lord blesses those who bless others, and I witnessed that firsthand. In the end, enough money was raised to pay for Holland's medical bills and replenish our savings so that we could still have a down payment for our first house. While this was a wonderful blessing, we were also grateful for the opportunity to get Holland's story out to more people and inspire others to lead better lives and truly value their blessings.

Notes

1. Alexis Kaufusi, "Holland Young's Battle," Alexis's Battle (blog), February 21, 2013, alexiskaufusi.blogspot.com/2013/02/holland-youngs -battle.html; complete post is available in Appendix C.

9

Happy Holland's Day

Before the race, at the very beginning of April, Holland had her first three-month follow-up MRI to see if the tumor had grown back. She was as stubborn and feisty as ever and refused to get sedated for the MRI. But despite the rocky start, the MRI went well and a week later at our chemo appointment, we got the results of the scan. We were a little nervous about it because we had no idea if the chemo was actually working or not. After discussing the chemo treatments, Dr. Shephard mentioned as an afterthought, "Oh, by the way the MRI the other day was clean."

"What?! This is great news!" It meant that all the pain and suffering of chemo was worth something. There was a light at the end of the tunnel, and we could make it through this because it was all working.

Right after the race, we took a little road trip down to Las Vegas for my nephew's wedding. We were grateful to spend a lot of time with family, and it was a great reminder of what is important in this life: family, first and forever. Holland was easily the life of the party. In fact, even people who didn't know her were taken back by the spirit and energy this little girl possessed. When you see a little girl dancing in the middle of a circle at a wedding to her favorite song, Taylor Swift's "I Knew You Were Trouble," you don't think, *This little pale-face girl is fighting for her*

life. You just see a little happy girl dancing at a wedding, and that night, that's all she was.

Holland's fourth birthday was on May 13 and she couldn't decide what kind of party she wanted to have. So we had a "Mario, Wreck-it-Ralph, Plants vs. Zombies" party—a general video game theme. Aleta worked extra hard to make it a special party, designing character cups, making a pin the head on the zombie game, and creating themed treats for everyone. Holland and her friends made candy race cars and even ran a Mario obstacle course. Watching this little girl eat cake, open presents, and run around in a Mario mustache with her friends, you never would have guessed that just the day before she had been in the ER for a slight fever and a cold that her weakened body was struggling to fight off.

Holland was doing well in her day-to-day life. When people asked how she was dealing with the chemo, I always told them, "I don't think she knows that this is any different than what other kids go through." May 31 marked one year since Holland's initial diagnosis. We decided to call it Happy Holland's Day. The school year had just ended and I didn't have to work, so we decided to spend the day together as family, letting Holland call the shots and doing whatever she wanted all day. This is how you celebrate Happy Holland's Day: Watch Mario clips on YouTube in your underwear for the morning activities. For lunch, a meal of baked beans, mashed potatoes, and pickles. After a quick trip to the store and a dreaded nap, it's Pizza Pie Cafe for dinner (even though we had just eaten there two weeks previously for her birthday). You must get balloon animals at dinner. Then you take a trip to the cemetery to see the Memorial Day flowers, and finally, you light smoke bombs and sparklers in the front yard. It was a pretty happy Holland's Day for all of us.

The truth was every day was Happy Holland's Day. We made the most of it. We knew that her life was a miracle and should be treated as such. How could a little four-year-old girl survive six brain surgeries and four months of chemo in one calendar year?

We were so glad and amazed at the fact that she was still with us after a roller coaster of a year. We had no idea that the real roller coaster was just about to begin.

The Tumor Comes Back

Because Holland was doing so well, we started to focus on buying our first house. In June, we found a house in Springville that we loved and made the final steps necessary to buy it. Buying a house can be a stressful situation, but doing so with a sick child is even harder. We were grateful for the help of a good friend and real estate agent, whose assistance was even more appreciated after Holland's six-month MRI at the end of June.

Because her last MRI had gone so smoothly, we anticipated that this would be much the same. And Holland did much better with the sedation this time. (I guess the sixth time's the charm.) Afterward, we planned to spend the weekend at my parent's house and just have fun with Grandma and Grandpa. That evening, however, we received a call from Dr. Shephard. She said, "I hate to do this kind of stuff over the phone, but the MRI revealed a bump in her resection cavity area and thickening in her lateral ventricle. In other words, it looks like the tumor has returned." She couldn't be sure of how far it had spread or what kind of tumor it was, so we would need to have a full spinal MRI on Monday and a spinal tap on Tuesday. Only then would we be able to see the full extent of the tumor's growth and whether or not it had spread or become more aggressive. She also asked that we come into her office the next day so she could show us the scans and explain in more detail what we could expect going forward.

When we met with Dr. Shephard, she showed us that the tumor was thick and beginning to spread, so it appeared to be fairly aggressive and most likely another mutation. They wouldn't be sure until they had all the scans and the tumor board met, but it looked like Holland would need to be on a much more aggressive chemo schedule. After the appointment, we decided to go to the nearby Hogle Zoo, which Dr. Shephard agreed to, since it was a good idea to just have some fun to break up all the scans Holland would be having that week. We ran into some friends there who asked how Holland was doing. When we told them the news we had just received, they looked shocked. "But she looks so happy and normal," they said. We knew with this new round of drugs that the "happy and normal" days would be coming to an end. This trip to the zoo might be the last time for a long time that she could just have fun in true kid fashion.

That Sunday I asked my father to help me give my family priesthood blessings. This was especially for Aleta, who was not taking this recent news well and felt very strongly that this time Holland was going to die. With my father, I placed my hands on Holland's head and we felt prompted to tell her that her Father in Heaven was mindful of her, that she would grow to be an adult, that she would serve as a missionary, and that she would have her own children one day. I also felt prompted to say that although she would go through much pain and suffering, she would be made whole. I then also gave Aleta a blessing that said the Lord was aware of her and was pleased with her strength and courage and example throughout this trial. It also said that she would be blessed to not see her children die and that she would greet them as they entered the celestial kingdom. I also blessed her with peace beyond the logic of this world. My father then gave me a priesthood blessing in which he blessed me with continual strength to lead and guide my family through this trial.

Holland had a spinal MRI on Monday, followed by a spinal tap on Tuesday to determine if there were any proteins or cancer cells in Holland's CSF. Right after the spinal tap we went up to the fourth floor to talk with Dr. Shephard, who had met with the tumor board. The MRI revealed a few growths on her spine—multiple tumors in her cerebellum, ventricles, and spine. The tumor board and Dr. Shephard had consulted a specialist in pilomyxoid astrocytoma at Johns Hopkins, and he suggested a chemo treatment. Holland would now be on a six-week cycle of four chemo drugs for the next eleven months. Three of the four drugs would be taken orally so we could administer them at home. But that ended up being more trouble than we thought and it required us to give them to her in the middle of the night for four nights. We needed to go to Primary's every two weeks for the other drug, vincristine, which she was already receiving but would continue taking at a higher dose. That night, we began what would be the final round of Holland's chemo treatments.

The Last Round of Chemo

Holland had been used to taking oral medications at home for some time and was starting to grow tired of it. She had orally taken Valium, Septra, Zofran, and steroids off and on for the last year, but she knew these chemo drugs were different. Just the smell of them was not something I would want to ingest. These drugs were so dangerous that we had to be extra careful with them. If she spilled them or spit them out, we had to wash and disinfect the area that the medicine touched. Imagine dealing with hydrochloric acid or another dangerous chemical and how careful you would have to be with it, taking care to handle it with goggles and gloves and lab coats. Now imagine force-feeding that to your four-year-old. This was especially hard because we had to give her the worst-tasting medicine every four hours for four days. This meant waking her up in the middle of the night and literally shoving poison down her throat, and if she spit it out, we would have to strip off her jammies and change her clothes and make sure that she still got enough of the drug.

We started this four-day round of chemo on the second of July, which meant she would be right in the middle of it on Independence Day. We had a big BBQ at my district office just north of LaVell Edwards Stadium where they did the Stadium of Fire every year. We had invited many friends and family members. Holland had eaten her dinner but afterward we had to give her the chemo medications. One of the meds, CCNU, was one of the biggest pills I had ever seen. We had to cut it into smaller pieces and feed it to her in her food. After dinner, we went upstairs to watch a movie while we waited for the fireworks to begin. Holland was sitting on my lap watching the movie when she started to say she didn't feel too good. I looked down at her just as she threw up all over me. We rushed her downstairs and into the bathroom to finish throwing up.

She had thrown up many times in the past, but this was different—she was screaming in pain, and her head was pounding. And since she had just taken the chemo drugs, all the vomit was toxic and needed to be cleaned immediately in case others breathed in the fumes or touched the vomit itself. So after cleaning everything up, Holland and I drove home in our underwear, missing the fireworks. The next day I went back to my office to deep clean the chairs and carpet that she had thrown up on. I had to bleach the chair, leaving a stain that is still there. Every time I see it, I'm reminded of that horrible night.

Aleta and I hated seeing Holland in pain, but that night was worse, knowing we had caused it by giving her the chemo. Also, this time we were surrounded by our family and friends, who weren't accustomed to seeing Holland so sick. Even though they knew she wasn't well, every time they saw her, she was the same spunky, energetic little kid. In contrast, we had become somewhat desensitized to Holland being sick, because we had seen so much of her suffering. But seeing the others' reactions reminded us how horrible a child's suffering is. Now they saw what her pain and illness really looked like. It's one thing to read about a kid having cancer online or to see it in a movie, but it's quite another to watch a little girl you know break down physically before your eyes.

A few days later we closed on our house, and to celebrate we went out to eat at Holland's favorite—Pizza Pie Cafe—and again, the chemo drugs got to her and she threw up all over our table and me. Again we had to clean everything as well as we could and inform the staff that helped us that she was on chemo and that they needed to sanitize everything she threw up on. It was painful for us to see her struggle to eat the foods she loved. Holland—who could eat an entire Happy Meal at less than a year old—was starting to lose her great appetite. And it showed as this round of chemo started to make her skinnier and paler than the other rounds had.

Holland was also starting to lose her happy and energetic personality. Even before she was diagnosed with the new tumor (around the time it had started to form again), we noticed that she had stopped smiling in pictures and would often get angry when people would try to talk to her. Despite this, we tried to help her enjoy her favorite things: we went to the weekly kids' movies at the Scera movie theater, we played at the park, we swam at the "big pool," we dressed up as cows for free Chick-fil-a day (again), we built a Toy Story car at Lowe's, and we even made a trip to Chuck E. Cheese's. She still managed to find joy in life, and for the most part, she was still happy, despite all the pain and suffering.

As Holland continued to get sicker, we were packing up our stuff, filling out paperwork, showing our house to prospective buyers, cleaning, and celebrating Dallin's birthday. Although it was a difficult time, we have a fond memory of trying to sell Holland on the idea of moving. We told her we had to move so she could have a room just for her toys, allowing her to get really big toys. She caught on fast. Every time we walked through a house she would say, "Is this where my toys will be?" After hearing this, our real estate agent bought her a huge stuffed dog when we closed. Before we brought Holland to walk through the new house, I put the big stuffed dog downstairs in the toy room. Holland was fairly unimpressed with most of the house, but when we walked into the toy room, she immediately ran over to the big dog and gave him a big huge hug. "It's a big fluffy dog," she squealed. "Everyone loves a big dog. I just love him! He's *so* cute!" This huge dog in this big toy room was her wish come true.

Moments like that were bright spots in our lives as Holland's future darkened. The night after her last chemo appointment, I was tucking her into bed as she told me, "I'm not taking that yucky medicine anymore."

Chapter 9

I tried to laugh it off and said, "We get to take a little break, but we have to keep taking it so the bad stuff in your head doesn't come back or get bigger."

But she resolutely repeated, "I'm not taking that medicine anymore."

I knew she had realized the medicine that we were giving her was what was making her so sick. I felt terrible and struggled to explain why she had to keep taking a medicine that wasn't helping her feel better and was actually making her feel much worse. I paused for a second and said, "Remember Daddy's grandma with the white hair?" (That's how she referred to Grandma Young.) "Remember how she died and went to live with Jesus a few month ago?" She nodded, remembering. "Well, if you don't take that medicine, the bad stuff could get worse and spread and you could die. And that would make Mommy and Daddy very sad, and we would miss you. And we don't want that to happen."

She just looked at me as I was obviously starting to tear up and get emotional. She simply stated, "I know, Daddy, but I'm not taking that medicine anymore." And then she kissed me and went to sleep.

I wonder now if she knew something then that I didn't. I wonder if the Lord had let her know what was ahead. I wonder if she was trying to warn me but seeing my emotions decided to hold back. I may never truly know what she knew in that moment, but I think she was just happy to never have to take that yucky medicine again.

10

The Week of Doctors

The last week of Holland's life will always be referred to as the Week of Doctors. It started off with our typical Monday chemo session. As we talked with the child life specialist, we learned that we had missed out on many of the things that most of the oncology kids did. She signed us up for the Hope Kids program and the Make-A-Wish Foundation. She also introduced us to the concept of "courage beads."

Primary's had a system of symbolic beads that you could collect for every part of the cancer treatment. A cat bead for every CT scan, a sun bead for every MRI, a bear bead for every steroid treatment, a black bead for when you had to be fasting from food, a red bead for every blood draw, and a yellow bead for every chemo treatment. There was a bead for everything, even if you spent a holiday in the hospital. We retroactively went back and got a bead for every part of Holland's treatment we could remember, and we left the hospital that day with a necklace that was over three feet long. We had never thought to do any of these programs because we had never thought of Holland as terminally ill. The nurses informed us that all the kids in oncology qualified for these and they gently reminded us that despite her attitude, Holland did have a life-threatening illness.

Meant for Heaven

We told Dr. Shephard that Holland seemed to be sicker than normal this last week. After listening to Holland's breathing, she told us that Holland might have a slight cold coming on, which was probably causing her to be sick on top of the chemo. She assured us there was nothing to be worried about. We left the chemo appointment and let Holland pick where she wanted to go for lunch. Naturally, she picked Pizza Pie Cafe. My parents came along and treated us to what would be Holland's last meal at her favorite restaurant. She loved it and didn't even get sick. She ate a whole plate of what she called the "crazy pasta" (radiatori) and enjoyed all the dessert pizza she wanted.

On Tuesday, we went to see our family pediatrician, Dr. Ryan, for Dallin's one-year checkup. He said that Dallin had a small dermoid cyst on his collarbone and referred us to a pediatric surgeon. He assured us that the cyst wasn't anything to be worried about but recommended that we get it removed. While we were there, we had the doctor give Holland a quick vision screening, since she had been squinting a lot and complaining of headaches. She failed the vision test that she had passed just a few months ago at her four-year checkup, so he referred us to a pediatric ophthalmologist.

On Wednesday, we went to the ophthalmologist, who did several vision tests with Holland. He informed us that the headaches and double vision were caused by a brain tumor that was putting pressure on her eyes—something he would be concerned about if he didn't already know she had a tumor. As it was, all we could do was to let the oncologists keep working on the tumor. Glasses at this point wouldn't help her, since she just needed the pressure removed and that couldn't happen while the tumor was there. We packed up to leave and decided to just go straight home, but when we got home Holland could hardly move because her head hurt so much and she began to throw up again. Waking up screaming and throwing up was just a part of life the last few weeks since we moved into the new house. But that day her pain seemed to be ratcheted up another notch.

Chapter 10

The Week of Doctors continued on Thursday as Aleta took Dallin to the pediatric surgeon while I stayed home with Holland. We watched cartoons all morning but she could barely stand to move, only getting up to go to the bathroom and throw up. When Aleta and Dallin came home, she said Dallin's cyst was not serious and that we could wait until the fall to remove it.

That afternoon, Aleta left to help out at a young women's day camp for one of our previous wards, and while she was gone, Holland could not sleep or hold down any food. While Holland tried to take a nap, I gave her a priesthood blessing—the second blessing in the last twenty-four hours—but she continued to struggle to fall asleep. Unable to relieve her pain or help her fall asleep, I fell to my knees in desperation, praying that she could get the sleep she so desperately needed, that she be made whole, that the chemo drugs would work and reduce the tumor. I pleaded with my Father in Heaven to take this trial away from her. I just wanted her to be able to sleep and wake up and be the little girl she had been before the chemo and the surgeries and the tumors. But it didn't work. She screamed in pain most of the day until Aleta came home. Together we got Holland and Dallin ready for bed. I gave her one more blessing before she went to bed. I blessed her that she would be able to sleep that night, and after two weeks of near-sleeplessness, she finally slept through the night.

To our great relief, the next morning she was happy and well rested and able to eat her breakfast and actually hold it down. It truly was a miracle. I felt as if the Lord had actually taken this trial from us, if only for a brief moment. I tentatively asked her, "Holland, since you're feeling better this morning, do you want to go to our movie?"

Her reply was so precious I hope I never forget it. She said, "I'd like to, but I'd probably need my throw-up bowl and I don't want to throw up at the movie. I'll just stay home with you." She was mature enough to understand that even though she wanted to go, it was probably best not to go out in public. She briefly helped me mow the lawn for the first time in our new house and she helped me kill a snake that we found in the grass. (For some reason, she really liked that.) Although she refused to take a nap, she was eating her meals and holding it all down. After dinner we visited our new neighbor to thank her for some treats she had made us. Holland was nice and polite (which was, lately, a bit out of character for her) but after a while she just wanted to go home. We didn't know it at the time, but this was the last time Holland would really talk with someone other than Aleta and me.

The Final Surgery

Holland went down to sleep very well that night after what had been her best day in weeks. I still gave her a blessing to help her fall asleep; Aleta and I knew that one good day did not mean things were all better. And sure enough, she had a much rougher night. She woke up and cried a couple times throughout the night, and around 6:30 a.m. she woke up and threw up all over her sheets. Aleta and I took her downstairs and laid her on the couch because she was screaming so loudly. I picked her up and could feel her having a seizure. We laid her down on the floor so she wouldn't bump into anything. Although the seizure only lasted a few seconds—five to ten at most—afterward Holland was unresponsive verbally. She would scream or cry or say "owwie," but that was it.

We had been through many scary experiences with Holland, but this seizure seriously frightened us; Holland had never had a seizure before. We called up the oncology department and asked them what we should do. They advised us to bring her to Primary's so they could have a look at her. We gathered a few things, not sure how long we would be staying there. We dropped Dallin off at my parents' house and made our way to Primary's, and on the ride up she occasionally screamed and cried but never spoke, seeming to be almost asleep but not quite. We arrived at the hospital mid-morning, and they set us up in a room and began to take her levels and vitals. After a little wait, Holland had another seizure, and afterward she continued to be unresponsive except to cry and scream. A neurosurgeon examined her and assessed that she had something putting pressure on her brain, but they weren't sure what. They took her down and gave her a CT scan and x-ray to get an image of what it could be.

After a while she began to throw up again and had another seizure. Looking at the scans, the neurosurgery team determined that she had some bleeding in her ventricles that was causing the shunts to clog, adding extra pressure to her brain. They decided that the shunt would need to come out and consequently scheduled her for surgery later that day. As they moved her into the E wing of the NTU (the only wing we hadn't been in at that point), Holland began having multiple seizures that lasted longer and longer. The neurosurgery team quickly bumped her surgery up to emergency status, and I had only moments to give her a priesthood blessing before she went into yet another surgery. They explained that they would need to remove her shunt and place external drains in to relieve the pressure, and once they opened her up, they might have a better idea as to what was causing the seizures.

We went back to the now very familiar home of the surgery waiting room and began to update our relatives on the situation. As we waited for news of the surgery, we talked about how this felt like we were entering into yet another unexplored roller coaster of life. Dr. Stevens, who performed the surgery since Dr. Burkes was out of town, came in after a relatively short time and invited us into what we called the "Bad News Room," a private room off of the surgery waiting area where they took you to tell you how the surgery had gone. But we had seen enough to know that if the surgery went well they didn't take you there—they just told you at your seat.

They ended up placing two external drains from her right and left ventricles due to the blood in her CSF—not a good sign. He assumed it had come from the tumors but said he'd have a better idea tomorrow when they did an MRI. Also, he told us the pressure in her head had been quite high—probably three times the normal amount. He hoped that since the pressure was now gone that the seizures would stop too, but it was only a hope, not a guarantee. They couldn't replace the shunt until her fluid cleared, so he expected that we could be in the hospital for ten to fourteen days—the last two weeks of my summer break.

We went back to the PICU to be with her, and although she was intubated as she had been many times before, this time she just looked lifeless and exhausted. Since Holland was still sedated and not anticipated to do much, Aleta decided to go pick up Dallin from my parents' house and head home for the night to gather up things for our latest hospital stay. My brother and his wife drove up to bring me dinner and some supplies to keep me through the night. Nurses fitted Holland's head with electrodes for an EEG to measure her seizure activity throughout the night. I got ready for bed, hoping to get some rest before what was no doubt going to be a long next day of recovery.

Despite the surgeries and the sedatives, she still woke up twice in the night and tried to remove the breathing tube. But other than that she had a good night with perhaps only one small seizure. The next morning, as Holland was going into her MRI, I decided to go up to the third floor and wait so I could listen to the piano music up there. The pianist was playing several songs from *Les Miserables*, one of my favorite musicals. As I sat and pondered the lyrics, they hit me with a new reality.

"You can take. You can give. Let him be. Let him live. If I die, let me die. Let him live."[1]

"I don't feel any pain. A little fall of rain can hardly hurt me now. You're here, that's all I need to know. And you will keep me safe. And you will keep me close. And rain will make the flowers grow. . . . You would live a hundred years if I could show you how."[2]

"I had a dream my life would be so different from this hell I'm living, so different now from what it seemed. Now life has killed the dream I dreamed."[3]

Like falling into a nightmare, these simple lyrics seemed to foreshadow a darker end to our story, one I had been avoiding. The realization came gradually: she might not bounce back from this round in the hospital. For the first time, I started to really consider that she might actually die and it hit me hard. I cried and cried as the pianist played and I thought, *There's a grief that can't be spoken. There's a pain that goes on and on. Empty chairs at empty tables. Now my friends are dead and gone.*[4]

The News

As Holland's MRI finished, Aleta arrived at the hospital and we went down to Holland's room, watching as the doctors removed her breathing tube and she started to wake up from her sedation. Normally Holland was quick to rebound from her sedation, and once she started talking, there was no stopping her. But this time she was awake but not alert, responding to questions with grunts or one-word answers like, "no," "ya," and "owwie." We sat with her as she gradually faded in and out of sleep. We talked with her nurse, chatting about things and catching up on how she was doing.

After a few hours, two doctors from oncology came in to talk about the results of Holland's MRI. Solemnly, they explained, "The tumor has spread to many different parts of her brain and has started to fill her ventricles. It has most likely mutated again and is now probably a stage 4 cancer tumor, called a glioblastoma. Because of the growth of tumors in her ventricles, we can't put the shunt back in without it clogging again, and the chemo and radiation can't work fast enough to keep up with the growth rate of the tumors. All of Holland's doctors will meet on Monday, when they get back, to discuss the options. In all honesty, it is not likely that she will live more than a month, and it could be as short as two weeks." With that they left us alone again.

I had played through this scenario in my head many times. What would I do if they told me she was going to die? Would I rage at the doctors or just cry or punch something? But as the doctors left, Aleta and I just sat there. All I could do was breathe as it all started to sink in: a cold, sinking, numb feeling. What were they telling me? Could this be true? No—I was just playing with her and killing a snake in the backyard two days ago. So many questions, so much disbelief. It felt surreal yet more real than anything I had ever experienced. It was like a really vivid dream I just wanted to wake up from but couldn't.

A little while later, Dr. Stevens and one of the neurosurgery residents came in. "Has oncology already been by to talk to you?" We said that they had, and Dr. Stevens explained that putting the shunts back in would just complicate things and that surgery-wise, there was nothing more they could really do. He had been on the phone with Dr. Burkes, who would be at the meeting on Monday to discuss what to do next. With a sober look at Aleta and me, he said, "Look, I'm not telling you what to do; she's not my child, but I've seen this too many times in my profession. They are going to give you the option to do radiation. Don't do it. It will just make her last days with you sick and miserable. It's too far gone. Just take her home and love her until she dies." And with that he left.

Notes

1. Claude-Michel Schönberg, Herbert Kretzmer, Charles Hart, and Webber Andrew Lloyd, "Bring Him Home," *Les Miserables* (MMO Music Group, 1986).
2. Claude-Michel Schönberg, Herbert Kretzmer, Charles Hart, and Webber Andrew Lloyd, "A Little Fall of Rain," *Les Miserables* (MMO Music Group, 1986).
3. Claude-Michel Schönberg, Herbert Kretzmer, Charles Hart, and Webber Andrew Lloyd, "I Dreamed a Dream," *Les Miserables* (MMO Music Group, 1986).
4. Claude-Michel Schönberg, Herbert Kretzmer, Charles Hart, and Webber Andrew Lloyd, "Empty Chairs at Empty Tables," *Les Miserables* (MMO Music Group, 1986).

11

The Comfort of the Lord

We proceeded to call our parents and family. I went upstairs to the parents' room to call my mom and dad, to explain what the doctors had told us. "They said, they said Holland . . ." As I started to say the words out loud they got caught in my throat, but through tears I proceeded, "The doctors have no hope left to offer. She's going to die." I could hear their tears on the other line and knew that this was just as hard for them to hear as it was for me to say. I also sent an email to the members of the Seventy who had worked with our family.

I just wanted to update both of you Brethren on her situation. When you gave her a blessing you said that she would live to adulthood and have a family of her own. And many blessings that I have given and promptings I have received have said the same thing: that she would live through this. However, at times like this, it becomes easy to doubt the promptings and blessings we have received. I feel like Abraham or Zechariah in the Bible who, when the Lord said their wives were with child, couldn't believe it. Though the Lord has told me many times and in many ways she will live through this and into adulthood, right now that just doesn't seem possible. In a blessing I gave her on Wednesday, the Lord said that she needed to go through this pain so that she could eventually be healed. I know that the Lord is still with us, but we feel awfully overwhelmed and helpless at times. It just feels that things keep getting worse, and we have yet to turn a corner when she starts to get better. I have questioned my faith in moments of darkness but then I am quickly reminded of the Lord's hand in my life and the miracles that we have already witnessed. I have often told others that I feel that we have gained more positive things then negative things through this experience; we have gotten stronger, and our faith and relationship with the Lord has increased. But right now I'm feeling very weak and questioning if the Lord can and will deliver on the promises He made to us. If she dies, we know that she will return to our Heavenly Father, and our temple sealing would allow us to see her again. But I would just wonder why He gave us such hope only to have her slip away.

One elder responded:

Dear Bryan and Aleta,

So sorry to hear about all of the challenges that Holland is having. The Lord obviously has great confidence in the two of you. "For whom the Lord loveth, he chasteneth."

As we all know, all blessings, healings, etc. come to pass in accordance with the Lord's will and in His own time and in His own way. Our responsibility is to exercise our faith, ask in faith, and bless in faith. We know that God can deliver Holland from these extreme challenges, if it is in accordance with His will. We remember the three Hebrew young men who were being cast into the fiery furnace. They stated that they had faith that God could deliver them from the fire. But they also added, "but if not" they would still have faith in Him.

This fast Sunday is another opportunity for all of us to exercise our faith and implore the Lord in behalf of Holland. My wife and I will join you in that fast and in those prayers. . . .

Chapter 11

May the Lord's healing influence continue to bless Holland and your family as you continue to persevere in faith during this most difficult time.

With love and admiration,
Your friend

With that email in mind and the news of the day beginning to wear us down, Aleta and I decided to go to the Salt Lake Temple to discuss with the Lord what we would do next.

We told the nurse where we were going and she said that she would watch over Holland while we were gone. Holland was mostly unresponsive and hadn't really changed from earlier that day. So Aleta and I changed into church dress and left to go to the temple. On our way down the hill from the hospital, one of Holland's favorite songs—"Trouble," by Taylor Swift—came on the radio, and we both started to cry. We took it as a sign or tender mercy that she agreed with our decision to go to the temple. As we drove to the hospital, I had the thought that I need to trust in the Lord more than the doctors. *If they say there is no hope and nothing can be done, the Lord will show me that there is hope and something can be done*, I thought.

We arrived at the temple and asked one of the matrons if we could dress in our temple robes and go straight to the celestial room. After hearing about our situation, she agreed and found someone to escort us up. There we found a small couch in the far corner and sat down. I held my wife's hand and looked at her in her temple robes. This was where we were supposed to be. I kissed her and bowed my head to pray, as did Aleta. When I receive answers to my prayers in the temple, it is often as if the Lord speaks to me through my thoughts. I think my silent prayer and then answers come quicker and more organized and clearly than my own thoughts. The voice has a different timbre to it, and although it comes through my own mind, I know it is not from me—the thoughts are not mine. They are from the Spirit of the Lord because they bring a transcendent peace to my mind.

I felt somewhat like Enos in the Book of Mormon who said, "I will tell you of the wrestle which I had before God" (Enos 1:2). As we sat in the temple, I wrestled before God, pleading with the Lord, "What should we do? Why is this happening? I know that you are a God of miracles and you have healed lepers, parted seas, and created worlds—surely you can heal my little girl. The doctors have no hope to offer us, but I know that You can heal her. You blessed her that she would live through this. Please, tell us what to do."

He immediately answered, as if cutting me off in mid-thought, "Your daughter Holland is going to die, and she will die much quicker than the doctors think. But this is my will and has been from the beginning. I knew that she would die and her death will bring many souls unto Christ."

I replied, "Then why would you tell me that she would not die, that she would be a mother and have children of her own? Why did you tell Aleta in a blessing that she would never see any of her children die and she would greet them in the celestial kingdom? If you knew that she would die the whole time, then why did you lie to me?!"

The Lord responded kindly but exactly,

I did not lie to you—you just did not understand what I was fully saying. You do not understand this life as I understand this life. When I say that she will live, I mean eternally. When I say that she will be a mother, I mean she will be a mother to worlds without end. When I say that she will be an adult, I mean that she is already an adult spiritually and that she will eventually grow to adulthood in the resurrection. When I say your wife will never have a child die, I mean spiritual death. When I say she will greet them in the celestial kingdom, I mean after the resurrection of all things. I did not lie to you, but I knew you would not understand what I was saying to you because you do not yet see things as I see things.

If I had told you more directly that your daughter would die, you would have begun to mourn her too soon and sheltered her, and she would have lost opportunities to grow and would have not been able to fully enjoy and learn from her life. I do not view life and death as the space from your first to your last breath. I view life as *eternal*. If My children will but trust in Me, they will have immortality and eternal life. I bless you to remember that you agreed to do this with Holland before this life.

And then, like a distant memory from somewhere else, I saw Holland and myself, standing at the feet of our Savior. Excitedly, I told Him, "We have an idea we have been studying. If I come down first as her dad and then she comes down as the child and gets sick, we can help people draw closer to Thee. We can be an example. She will teach people on that side of the veil and I would serve people on earth, and we would show people how to turn to God in times of trial."

Christ looked at us and said, "This is a good plan. It will bring many people unto me on both sides of the veil and will help each of you grow. But it will be harder than you think. There will be much pain and suffering and grief and sorrow with this plan, but if you endure it well, it will bring to pass much good."

And we—not knowing anything of death, pain, cancer, grief, and suffering—gladly said, "If it will bring souls unto Thee, we are willing to take on these challenges." We said that naively, just trusting that what Christ said was true. We trusted Him and wanted to serve Him in bringing souls unto Him in any way we could.

The memory faded from view, and Heavenly Father continued, "I told you from the very beginning that she may die from this, but if you trust in Me everything will be okay. And now is the time for her to die."

I replied to the Lord, "But you told me last December in this very room that if it had not been for my faith and the faith of my friends and family, she would have died last May. What has changed between then and now? My faith has only grown from that point, so how is my faith not enough to allow her to live now when it was then?"

He kindly responded,

Meant for Heaven

If you had walked out of the temple last May and not trusted in what I had told you and not had the faith to grow from this trial, it would have begun to make you bitter and callous to My will. You would have turned your back on the very faith that was keeping her alive, and I would have had to bring her back home at that point because the plan that you presented to my Son would have failed due to your lack of faith. And her continued life would have only served to make you more angry and upset. But because you left the temple that day trusting in Me, you were able to build her up with optimism and faith that not only allowed her to grow and heal, but also allowed you to grow and heal, and that spirit spread to your family and friends. And so I granted you fourteen more months to allow that spirit of faith to continue to grow and spread to more people. And look at the lives you have touched. Think of all the people who learned selflessness by serving you and donating of their time and money for the many fund-raisers you held. Think of all the people who have been inspired by the thoughts you have posted online. Think of each doctor and nurse who was affected by your family's hope and optimism in times of trial. Think of each ward member who showed up to church and was inspired to keep coming to church because they saw young Holland happily showing up to Primary despite having just had brain surgery days before. Think of every testimony that you bore in personal quiet conversations with friends, family members, and coworkers. This is just a taste of the lives that you have brought closer to your Savior because of this trial.

Because of your faith, I have extended her life, but now because of her faith, I must end her stay on this earth. She has completed the mission I sent her to do. But now your mission in many ways is truly beginning. She has completed her part of the plan with courage, faith, enthusiasm, and infectious energy that has been a light to all who knew her. Now it is up to you—as you not only agreed to but also helped to plan before this life began—to continue to bring souls unto Me. Trust in Me and I will give you continued opportunities to learn and grow from this trial and to help others do the same.

You will be a light to those who know you and you will be an example to them of how to trust in the Atonement of my Son. If you doubt not and fear not, you and Holland and all of your family will continue to be the means to bring many souls unto Me. Now go and be with your daughter as she is prepared to enter back into My presence. Now that you are prepared to let her go, she can finally be made whole as you have blessed her so many times to do.

And with that I opened my tear-filled eyes and looked at my dear wife, who also was crying. I simply said, "She's going to die." We embraced and cried some more and she looked at me as if she had been told the same thing. We got up from the celestial room and as we left we were greeted by a large painting by Carl Bloch of Christ with a young child in a plain white tunic. I have seen that painting many times before and many times since, but in that moment, we both agreed that the child looked similar to Holland. We took that as a sign that Christ was with our family and He would not leave us. Although Holland would die, He would welcome her into His loving arms and she would know such great peace.

I went into the dressing room to change and tears began to fill my eyes, not because I was sad, but because of how humbled I was by that temple experience. The Lord had reassured me that my life was pleasing to Him and that if I trusted in this plan I would be able to be with Holland again. I now knew that to be true, which gave me the faith I needed to let her go. As we left the temple, we quietly entered Holland's name into the prayer role of the temple, not so that she would be healed, but so that she would truly be made whole as she had long been promised.

12

The Final Good-Byes

When we arrived back at Holland's hospital room, she looked just as lifeless as she had when we left her. The nurse said that she had stirred a little bit and said a few things but nothing major. Moving to the bed, I hugged Holland and kissed her, knowing that her fight would soon be over. Then I left to make some phone calls to family and also to our previous bishop, Bishop May, to make funeral arrangements. I told him that Holland had not been given long to live, that the doctors had said two to four weeks but we felt it would be much sooner. He was floored, since he had just seen her in Primary two weeks earlier. Although we had just moved out of his ward, he graciously agreed to host the funeral at our old ward building where she had grown up.

Meanwhile, Aleta stayed with Holland in her room, holding her hand and singing Primary songs. One of Holland's favorite songs was, "Holding Hands Around the World," and Aleta sang it to her:

> There are children singing all around the world,
> Happy voices ringing out the joyful word:
> We are children glowing with the gospel light,
> Standing tall, walking strong, choosing right.
> There are children leading out in ev'ry land

Who believe in keeping all the Lord's commands.
Like the stripling warriors, we go forth in faith,
For we know that the Lord is our strength.

We are children holding hands around the world,
Like an army with the gospel flag unfurled.
We are led by His light,
And we love truth and right.
We are building the kingdom of God.

There are children sharing all around the world,
Leading other children to the gospel fold.
With the strength of youth, we do the Father's work.
With our hearts and our hands we will serve.
We are cov'nant children with a gift to give.
We will teach the gospel by the way we live.
With each word and action, we will testify:
We believe, and we serve Jesus Christ.[1]

As Aleta sang, Holland started to get goose bumps. Seconds later, she started to seize again. By the time I got there, the room was full of doctors and nurses. They decided to put the breathing tube back in and give her more anti-seizure medications. Although it would be several hours before she was pronounced dead, Aleta and I felt that this was the moment her spirit left her body. She just felt different—the fight was gone and she was lifeless.

Aleta decided to go home to my parents' house to help put Dallin to bed. Before she left, the attending physician of the PICU approached us and asked, "Before you leave, what are your wishes?" We weren't quite sure what she meant, and she explained, "In the event that something happens and Holland takes a turn for the worse, we need to document if it is your wish to allow her to die or to keep her alive through artificial means." We talked and decided that we wanted to keep her alive until Monday, when we could talk with all of her doctors to see what the plan would be going forward. After documenting our wishes, Aleta left, and I was alone with Holland. Looking at her lifeless, spiritless body, the realization began to sink into my heart that I would never hear her voice again and would never see her smile and she would not be there to watch cartoons with when I came home. The doctors came in to put the breathing tube in, and I decided that I didn't need to see that and so I stepped out of the room.

When I came into the PICU waiting room, my aunt and uncle were there. I have never been extremely close with any of my aunts or uncles, but in that moment they were the greatest sight I had ever seen. I embraced them both so tightly, and tears began to flow. This was the first physical support of love I had gotten from anyone besides Aleta since this whole thing began on Friday. I let out every emotion that had been bottled up inside me on my unsuspecting aunt and uncle. In that moment they were answers to prayer, the family I needed to release all that was building up inside of me to, and I was extremely grateful.

A little while later my mom and dad came with my sister and her husband, and they joined us upstairs in the third floor lobby. We embraced and chatted about serious things but also lighthearted things as well. I don't remember all we talked about, but I remember laughing, which felt so good. I also told them some of the things the Lord had revealed to me in the temple. I just enjoyed being with family and not thinking about my dying little girl that lay in her bed downstairs. While we talked, I had received a couple phone calls from an unknown number. When I finally picked it up, it was from one of the doctors in the PICU. They wanted me to come down as soon as I could. I told my family to wait while I checked in with them.

While I was gone, Holland had had more seizures, so they decided to run a CT scan to see what was causing them. The images of the results showed that in the hours since her MRI that morning, her entire brain had been taken over by the aggressive tumor. They said for all intents and purposes, she was brain dead and at this point the machines were keeping her alive. Grimly they asked me, "What do you want to do?"

"I'll obviously want to discuss this with my wife," I told them. When she picked up the phone, I gave her the news and we both decided to take her off of life support as soon as Aleta could make it back.

My sister stayed with Dallin as he slept, and Aleta joined my family at Holland's bedside. Although it was not strictly necessary, I felt impressed to give her a blessing of release, to free her spirit from her body and officially hand her over to her Father in Heaven and thank Him for the time He gave us with her. So with my father, brother, and brother-in-law, we placed our hands upon her head and gave her a blessing of release. I don't recall everything that was said, but I recall blessing her to leave in peace and enter quickly into the waiting arms of her Savior Jesus Christ. I blessed her that she would continue to be a part of her brothers' and sister's lives, which was interesting because Dallin was our only other child at the time.

I praised her for the joy she had brought to the world, and I told her of the love that was and would always be felt for her. I will never forget the peace in that room, which was greater than I had ever felt before.

Because another child in critical condition had just been life-flighted into the PICU, they asked if they could delay pulling her breathing tube. We told them we were in no hurry to see our daughter die and that they should devote their full energy to the other child. Each one of my family members said their good-byes, my mother leaving last of all and giving Holland a kiss on her forehead. Aleta and I were alone with Holland again. Her skin was ice cold and her temperature had steadily dropped to 93 degrees Fahrenheit. Other parents walked by and looked in to our room. I saw their faces and knew the look that they gave us, because I had given others that look many times myself. *At least my kid doesn't have it as bad as that kid,* I'd think as I walked the hallways of the PICU and saw other parents sitting by their dying children. At Primary Children's, there's always someone who has it worse than you do, and it puts your trials in perspective. But today I was on the other end of those stares. We were the family that was giving other families hope and added perspective. At this moment, no one else in the hospital could look at us and think, *I wish I could trade places with them.* We officially had it worse than anyone else in the hospital as we waited for the doctors to pull our child's last tie to this mortal world.

Finally a doctor and a nurse stood quietly in the doorway, prepared to pull the breathing tube. We nodded and moved back as they removed the shunts and tubes and wires that had kept her alive for the last several hours. They warned us that because she had shown the ability to take a few breaths on her own that she may struggle to try and breathe when they pulled the tube, which might prolong her life for a few hours at most. But we knew that her fight was gone. She had been blessed with peace and was ready to let go. At 1:30 a.m., they pulled the breathing tube and invited us to lay with her. Aleta laid on her right side and I on her left. For the next fifteen minutes we each held her hands, and I laid my hand on her chest to feel her heart beat. It was slow and then began to speed up, faster and faster. At one point it felt like it would beat right out of her chest but then it peaked and began to slow again. Her heartbeats came slower and slower until it was hard to feel her heart beat at all. Finally, at

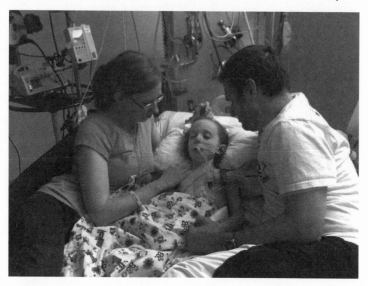

1:45 a.m., her tiny heart beat its final beat and the machines gave off a steady monotone hum and then an alarm went off, indicating to the nurse that she had died. She turned off the alarm and the attending doctor declared the time of death to be 1:45 a.m. on Sunday, August 4, 2013.

The doctor and nurse quietly left the room, giving us some time to be alone with her. I got up from the bed and let go of her icy fingers. My heart shattered as I looked down at the corpse that now lay on that bed, the body that was not my vibrant young four-year-old. The color and the life had completely left her body. In that moment I began to sob harder than I had ever allowed myself to cry. This was the pain and anguish that I had dreaded. My soul ached as I looked down—it was over. There was nothing we could do to bring her back. Between heart-wrenching sobs, I looked at Aleta and asked, "How do we move on? How can we ever be happy again? How can I go to work or a football game or watch TV and ever expect to feel joy again?" Any chance of happiness died with Holland—it was all lost, and it was not coming back. Without a doubt, this was the greatest pain I have ever felt and hope to ever feel. Quite literally a very real part of my own soul died, and I was not sure I could bear it. But with the help of my wife, who reminded me what I still had left to live for, I was able to regain my composure. We had both known this moment was coming, and once it was here, it was both surreal and more real than anything we'd experienced.

We very solemnly left the hospital and headed out to the parking lot. As we started up the car, I reached into my pocket for my phone but couldn't feel it. My mind and heart began to spin into a panic—this wasn't simply a mobile calling device; this phone had every photo I had taken of Holland for the last three years. It contained her voice, her image, her videos. If I was going to remember what she was like, I would need this one material possession. I frantically looked all over the car and uttered a very heartfelt plea to the Lord to help me to find it. We decided to go back to the hospital and retrace our steps. These steps brought us back into the room where it had all ended. We told the nurse that we needed to go back in and look for my phone, and she said she had been cleaning the room and hadn't seen it but would allow us to have a look. We came back in and saw our daughter there as lifeless as the cold, sterile bed on which she lay. She seemed no more alive than the instruments on the walls. That was not my daughter—that was a body and nothing more. My daughter was gone, but she was at peace, and that thought allowed me to go back to the car with no phone in hand. The memories of who she was were not as important as the knowledge of who she is now. Aleta called my phone one more time as we drove away, and I reached down and discovered it under my seat. I knew the Lord had given me this to realize this lesson: that Holland is more than the memories we made. She is a living spirit that I will never lose again. I have not lost her, for I know where she is. She is with my God and my Savior. I have not lost her, though I miss her more than I can describe. She is not lost, for she is mine, but more importantly she is the Lord's, and He will never let her go until we meet again.

Notes

1. Janice Kapp Perry, "Holding Hands Around the World," *Friend*, July 2002; used with permission.

13

The Next Day

We arrived at my parents' house around 4:30 a.m. We were physically and emotionally spent, though it wasn't a particularly restful night. I heard Dallin wake up a couple of hours later, so I quietly rolled out of bed to let Aleta sleep. As I picked up Dallin from his crib, I was reminded that life keeps going on. This little boy could not afford for me to check out. Hours after his sister died, this one-year-old little boy didn't know what was going on. He just knew his diaper was wet and he needed breakfast. I took him upstairs, and for a moment he just embraced me. We quietly hugged as a father and son for several moments. Even though he couldn't know what was going on, it seemed as if he was reaching out and comforting me, as if to say, "Dad, it's going to be okay. I'm still here. I still love you, and I still need you."

In the hours that followed, my family members slowly started to wake up. As it so happened, my sister and her family were up from Las Vegas, so the house was full of aunts and uncles and cousins and grandparents. As everyone woke up and heard the news, we all just cried in silence, knowing that nothing could be said. Every now and then someone would chime in with a memory or story of Holland, but we all just seemed dazed as to what to say or do.

When Aleta woke up, she asked me, "Well, what do you want to do today?"

I said, "It's Sunday, and I need some sense of normalcy. Let's go to church." She agreed, and we discussed which ward we wanted to attend. We could have gone to the ward at Primary's, my parents' ward, or our old ward, but I thought, *No, if I want to feel normal, I need to go to* my *ward.* And so we changed into our church clothes and drove down to our new ward, which we had only attended twice before. Even though we didn't know a soul in that ward, we felt that it was our home now and where we needed to be.

We stopped briefly at our new house, which felt so empty now with no sounds of Holland to fill the box-lined rooms. Aleta's friend had kindly stopped by our house that morning to do the dishes and clean up, and apparently she had also called our new bishop to tell him that Holland had died. When we got to the church building, we took our seats in the upper right side and were immediately greeted by all three members of the bishopric. They extended their condolences and amazement that we had actually come to church. I told them that we just needed to feel like it was actually Sunday and our lives were somewhat normal. The first counselor, Brother Anderson, with tears in his eyes, told us that the hard part was that our church records had just come in and they were going to read them from the pulpit to welcome us into the ward. "Would it be okay if I read Holland's name and announced that she has just passed away? It would show that Holland will always be a member of this ward, just like your family." We said that would be fine with us, and the bishopric returned to the stand.

As church began, we watched the unfamiliar faces come in and take their seats. They were unaware of who we were or what we had just gone through. They were probably just concerned with normal Sunday church things like preparing lessons, keeping kids still, and quieting the hunger pains of a fast Sunday. They had no idea of the pain behind our eyes. They had no idea that this small family of three was actually now an incomplete

Chapter 13

family of four. I don't remember what the opening hymn was, but I remember struggling to sing every word. Each line reminded me that we were going through the toughest trial of our lives. Brother Anderson stood to make normal Sunday announcements such as ward parties, new callings, and releases. And then, taking a deep breath as if preparing to leap from a cliff, he announced our names and invited us to stand. As we sat back down, tears streamed down his face as he announced that our daughter, Holland, had passed away earlier that day. His own grief and sympathy was difficult for me to watch—he had never met her and didn't know any of us. But I began to realize that this would be hard for everyone who knew us. I could not simply wallow in my own grief and pain—I knew I must work to comfort others as well.

As we partook of the sacrament, the bread and water were a relief to my lips. It was like a traveler taking a long drink after a hike through the desert. If ever there was a time that I needed to take the name of Christ upon me, it was this time. If ever there was a time that I needed to know that Christ had felt my grief and pain, it was now. If ever I needed His Spirit to always be with me, it was at this very moment. I have taken the sacrament thousands of times in my life, but this was one of the most necessary times for me to take it. In my mind I thought, *This is why I felt the need to come here.* The bread and water were the solace to my soul that would give me the strength to make it through the week ahead. They were not only the relief that I needed after a weary hike, but they were the fuel to take me through the next leg of this journey. I felt the strength that they offered, and I was thankful for the atoning sacrifice that my Lord and Savior Jesus Christ had offered for me and for Holland so that we could not only live again but so that we could be made perfect through Him and be forgiven for all our faults and sins. This bread and this water would be what I needed to get me back to where she now was. Without the Atonement, we truly would have lost her.

While Brother Anderson tearfully gave his testimony of the gospel to begin the testimony portion of the meeting, the Spirit told me that I needed to bear my testimony to this congregation of relative strangers. I was unsure of what to say, but I knew it was what the Lord needed me to do. As soon as the invitation was extended to come up and bear testimony, I walked up to the pulpit. I don't remember everything I said, but I remember looking at the clock for a while and saying, "My name is Bryan Young and my daughter, Holland, died ten hours ago." I then bore my testimony of some of the things the Lord had taught me in the temple the day before. I briefly shared some of the history of her tumors and the journey our family had taken. I knew that this was the Lord's will and that He had strengthened us and would continue to strengthen us. I had felt her last heartbeat, but I knew that she was not gone, but that she had merely transitioned. I remember closing in the name of my Friend and Savior, Jesus Christ. The eyes of the members of the ward were mixed with awe and tears and shock that someone would stand up in front of so many people and speak after having gone through so much. I didn't know why I did, but I knew that the Lord needed me to.

Many of the people who were there have since told of how meaningful that experience was to them. Some talked about seeing the Light of Christ emanate from me; others talked about the strength that it gave them to make it through their own trials. President Fisher, our stake president, later told us that word had spread throughout the stake of the things I had said, and it was helping people maintain their faith through their own large bumps in the road. After the meeting, a slew of people—absolute strangers at the time, but now close friends—came up and introduced themselves to us. It was a bit overwhelming to start in a new ward under such circumstances, but the ward lifted us and welcomed us with open arms.

We went home and put Dallin down for a nap, thinking of the life he would have without his big sister. He was now an only child. Slipping quietly out of his room, we entered Holland's room and sat, looking at her bed and thinking of all the memories that would never be made in this house. After some tears, we decided to call some of our best friends who happened to be

Chapter 13

in town that weekend, visiting from Alaska. We had canceled plans for a BBQ with them on Friday when Holland was in the hospital, but we did want to see them before they left that night.

Our visit with them was perfect—just what we needed. We had been thrown into a new life without Holland, and spending time with our friends provided a nice mix of familiar faces and stories with this stark new life. They brought the Spirit and love that we needed as well. A year later, our friend shared with us the pages from his journal entry of that day and they were a great opportunity to see the same experience through someone else's eyes. His words are as follows:

> When we got home, we saw on Facebook that Bryan . . . had posted that Holland's situation had worsened. Tumors were growing fast, and the supposed two-week hospital stay to drain brain pressure had changed to a "two weeks to live" diagnosis. This blindsided us. We thought she was the miracle girl with unusual spunk and energy that defined her as a cancer defeater. She'd battled through chemo, and we thought she would live to be an inspiring girl who outsmarted cancer.
>
> Bridget and I went to sleep that night with heavy hearts. We were determined to go to Primary Children's Hospital to visit them and share our love. I texted Bryan the next morning first thing and told him, "Bryan, we understand if you guys don't want visitors, but if you're up for it, Bridget and I really want to come visit. I fly out tonight. We're praying for you, and I am fasting for all four of you today."
>
> I jumped on Facebook and the first thing I saw was a status update from Bryan saying . . . she peacefully passed away. It floored Bridget and me. We consider the Youngs among, if not, our closest friends. We have loved them and prayed for them and visited them and had amazing heart-to-heart talks. We click so well as couples and feel as though we shared in their burden. . . . It was a morning of nonstop tears, crying, grieving, and memories.
>
> We went to church and we left after sacrament meeting. . . . As we were driving to the freeway, Bryan called. They were

at their new home . . . and wanted us to come visit. We had no idea what to expect, but we drove straight to their house.

Bridget and I talked of how we hoped to help. We wanted to provide some normalcy, help around the house if we could, and offer a shoulder to cry on. We were a mess ourselves though, and thought we'd be a mess. We walked to their doorstep hand in hand not knowing what to say or what was waiting for us on the other side of the door.

We had spent most of the day beside ourselves with grief. I personally felt little peace and ached for our friends and their beautiful Holland. We were met, though, with two people who had come to accept the will of God. They were by no means happy. We shared tears, memories, and they told us of their final minutes with Holland, right to the last heartbeat. However, they exuded faith and acceptance of God's plan for them, telling of numerous tender mercies along their journey, both small and large. They held their composure well for the most part, often better than us. It was so apparent, though, that they loved this girl with all their heart. They gave themselves to her. They offered their souls to serve and love her during her darkest times.

We prayed together, [and] they gave us a baby gift and then offered us a shirt of Holland's that she loved that says "Big Sister." According to Bryan and Aleta, she had treasured the shirt and loved being a big sister to Dallin. They offered it to us in tears. We reluctantly left, not wanting to break the spirit that permeated our conversation. I also sensed they didn't want us to leave because it meant they had to go back and face reality. They had to meet with the morgue and handle other awful chores leading up to the funeral. After a typical Smith/Young drawn-out good-bye, we left feeling a little bit of closure and peace.

I'll be returning to Utah for the funeral and meeting up with Bridget. We know it will be a thoughtful service and will hopefully bring peace to all, but most especially Bryan, Aleta, and their families. I worry about them and how they may adjust to life after the funeral. I know their faith will carry them, but it doesn't get rid of my worry.

Chapter 13

After our friends left, we went back to my parents' house and spent the rest of the day meeting and talking with more friends and family. Messages continued to pour in through phone calls, text messages, and Facebook posts and comments. There was just an overwhelming flow of support from all our friends and family, which was exactly what we needed to get us through the day. Little though we wanted to, we also started making funeral plans, calling funeral homes and cemeteries.

14

Holland Was Not Gone

That night, I started to realize how impossible sleep was going to be. I didn't sleep well for several weeks after Holland died. My mind just kept racing with thoughts of what if, and what will never be, and "how do we move forward?" My mind was just so full of pain, grief, hope, peace, love, support, and every emotion under the sun—and it was hard to turn them off. That night we were at my parent's house and I managed to get three hours of sleep to go with the two hours I had had the day before. I woke up around 4:30 a.m., unable to settle my mind.

I went upstairs and read scriptures and watched videos and looked at pictures of Holland. As the sun started to rise, I went outside on the front porch to watch the dawn of a new day without Holland. This was the first full day without her, and, in many ways, it was the start of the rest of our lives going forward. As the sun shone on my face, I bowed my head in prayer and asked Heavenly Father to continue to lift me up so that I could be the support that others needed me to be. In response He spoke to me and said many things He had told me before and reminded me that this was the plan. He then said that Holland was desirous to speak to me. I did not know what that meant but it brought me peace.

And then in my mind, I heard her voice. It was so clear it was nearly audible. Like Paul said of his vision in the New Testament, "whether in the body, or out of the body, I cannot tell" (2 Corinthians 12:3). Regardless of where this voice originated from or how I heard it, I knew that I was hearing it and I knew that it was her voice. It was quiet, high, and small. She said,

> Daddy, it's me. I'm with the Savior, and He is everything people have described Him to be and more. He offers such love and comfort. I was a bit confused at first but then Uncle Nelson [Aleta's brother who passed away] came to me and helped me find my way around this place. He is kind of in charge of helping new spirits figure out the spirit world. This place is beautiful and a lot of fun. People here are very busy preparing for Christ to come to earth again, and there is a lot to be done on both sides. Dad, it's hard to see you be so sad when I know that things are fine. Don't be sad for me. This is where I need to be. This was part of the plan, so please just keep trusting in the Lord and the plan that we made will work out just as we planned it.

As she spoke, her voice began to mature and it sounded more like Aleta's voice than Holland's. She was speaking much more sophisticatedly than she ever had here on earth.

> Death did not hurt nearly as much as the cancer did. It was like just letting go of all that pain and suffering and immediately being filled with peace. I have also met a little girl that is part of our family. She is my sister and she is excited about the time when she can come down and be a part of our family. Don't be sad—they are taking care of me, and I am safe and happier than I have ever been. If you want to visit me, don't go to my grave; that's just where my body is. If you want to visit with me, go to the temple: that is where I will be and that is where I will be able to best speak with you. Please tell Mom the same thing. Let her know that if she wants to talk to me, she can, just like you did, if you show her how. I have to go. Like I said, things are very busy, and Uncle Nelson has

Chapter 14

some things he needs to show me. I love you and Mommy and Dallin, and I will always be with you. Bye, Daddy.

And with that I opened my tear-filled eyes. Light spilled from over the mountains as the sun began to rise, much brighter than it had when I had closed my eyes. I was so overcome by what had just happened that I could hardly move. After a few moments I looked over to see Aleta standing at the door with Dallin in tow. She came outside and saw my red eyes and knew that I had just been crying. "Are you doing okay?" she asked.

"I'm doing better than I have in a long time. I just got to hear her voice."

Aleta seemed confused, "What do you mean?"

"I was praying and the Lord said that Holland wanted to speak to me and so she did." I described all the things that she had told me about the temple and Nelson and Christ and the work they were doing. "And then she told me that she would talk to you. You just need to say a prayer and ask for it and then be still and quiet and the thoughts will come to your mind. Just trust that they are from her and not simply your own thoughts."

And so I took Dallin, and Aleta sat on the porch and began to pray. I left her alone, but when I came back her eyes were also filled with tears. She told me that she, too, had heard Holland's voice in her mind. For her it sounded like the mature older voice that hers had eventually changed into. She said that Holland told her that she was a good mommy. This made her cry because she had been concerned that she was too hard on her. That she was too strict. But Holland told her that she helped her to learn and that Aleta had needed to be strict or Holland would have never learned many of the things that she did. She also talked about going to the temple and about being with Nelson.

People can say what they will about us hearing voices or just telling ourselves what we want to hear, but I know on that morning we heard her—we felt her. We both talked about feeling a "spiritual hug" from her—not a physical touch of her hand, but a warmth that embodied all around us. I know that this was what

103

needed to happen and that it was her voice and her presence. Since that time I have gone to the temple every week to hear her voice. I don't always get to hear her the same way because she is busy and I can't just summon her when she has other responsibilities. But the Lord has taught me that I will have visitations from her as I need them, not as I want them. He has also taught me that if I want to see her or feel her physically, then I do not fully understand who she is. I need to stop wishing she was more like me, and I need to start being more like her. I have a body of flesh and a body of spirit, but she has only a body of spirit. If I focus on my spiritual communication, I can find her, but if I'm expecting a physical experience, I can't feel her near. I have learned to develop my spiritual ears, eyes, mouth, hands, and mind. She was with me that day and she is with me still.

15

The Week That Followed

The week that followed was filled with visits and tears. Have you ever cried to the point where your eyes began to sting, like your body ran out of tears so they just start sending fire out of your eyes? All week our eyes were red and puffy, but there were still smiles on our faces. Slowly all of our family came into town. Aleta's parents came and stayed with us, which really helped with Dallin. They watched him while we visited and planned with other family members.

My sister came into town and helped sort through all of Holland's things, separating them into piles: things to keep, things to donate, things for Dallin or a future sister. We were glad to go through her things quickly, as other parents who had lost a child had told us the longer you wait, the harder it becomes. We also decided to give most of her toys and clothes away to her friends and family members so that they could each have a keepsake to remember her by. This was a great blessing to us, since it freed our home from many painful memories and filled others' homes with joyful ones. My sister and her husband also very kindly offered to pay all of the funeral home costs. Since we had just bought a home, our savings were decimated. We were prepared to cover other costs, but they would end up being covered by more donations. In the end, we paid next to nothing for all of the funeral and burial expenses. The kindness and generosity of others was greatly appreciated.

That week we also went back to Primary's to thank the doctors, nurses, and staff who worked with Holland. Many of them were shocked when they heard the news; she had just been in for a chemo appointment a week prior and had seemed fine to them. Her oncologist couldn't believe the scans when she saw them—she thought there had to have been a mix-up because the tumor had spread so aggressively.

For days I had been pondering Holland's obituary. After much thought and prayer, I was able to come up with this:

> Holland Gwen Young peacefully passed away at Primary Children's [Hospital], in the arms of her parents, on Sunday, August 4, at 1:45 a.m. After a fourteen-month-long battle with brain tumors, Holland's body finally succumbed to her cancer. Although Holland had [seven] brain surgeries and seven months of chemo, her love of life remained the same. She was a determined, bright, smart, and spunky four-year-old that loved everything about life. Her big infectious smile made everyone laugh. She loved to take in as much of this world as she could because her spirit knew that her time here was short. Holland didn't really have favorites because she loved everything and everyone. However, some of her top pastimes included watching cartoons, going to the movies and eating bucket after bucket of popcorn, going to the "big pool" (Seven Peaks Waterpark), building forts, swinging on swings, jumping on trampolines, reading stories, playing on the iPad, playing Super Mario Brothers on the Wii, and "scary things" (Halloween, monsters, ghosts, skeletons, Plants vs. Zombies, Killer Pianos, etc.). She loved playing with people of all ages, and especially loved playing with her many friends, her thirty-four cousins, her eleven aunts, and ten uncles, her grandma and grandpa with the chickens and also her grandma and grandpa with the puppies. Most of all, especially in the last few months of her life, she just wanted to spend time with her one-year-old brother, Dallin, her mother, Aleta, and her father, Bryan. All those who knew her and even many that did

not, but whom she influenced, will miss Holland in this life. We know that her spirit lives on and that she is on the other side continuing to spread the Gospel of peace, joy, love, and hope with her departed family and her Brother and Friend, Jesus Christ.

That week we also took on the task of planning the funeral. The real challenge for me was delegating anything. I wanted to sing the songs, I wanted to give the talks, I wanted to offer the prayers, because I was the only one who knew her well enough to truly portray who she was. Aleta and my sister tried to convince me that it would be harder to do those things than I thought. But in the end, I realized that I needed to share the opportunities to serve Holland by remembering her with all those who cared about her. My sister took Aleta and I to get brand new yellow clothes to wear to the funeral. (Holland's favorite color was yellow, and we asked everyone to wear yellow to the funeral.) My nephew's wife gave me a haircut. So many people donated time, resources, and money to support us. Through these acts of service, I realized that the Lord was very mindful of every aspect of this funeral. This would be an opportunity to help many people to feel the Spirit in a way they had not yet felt it.

Aleta and I were beginning to feel the effects of not eating or sleeping enough. We had both lost between five and ten pounds in the week since she died. We were running out of energy, but we could feel that the fasting and prayers of our loved ones were sustaining us. It was a very real feeling, when our strength was gone, to feel that angels were all around us on both sides of the veil. Every meal, every flower, every call, message, or donation was from one of the Lord's living angels. But when we were beyond exhausted, the strength to move came from the Lord's ministering angels that were round about us to lift us up. On our right hand and on our left, behind us, and in front of us—every move we made that week was accompanied by the unseen beings of our Lord, and we could feel their very real support.

Meant for Heaven

The viewing was held the evening before the funeral. The funeral director had done a great job not only to remove much of the stress of funeral planning but also to bring the peace that was needed for the entire event. We gave more hugs and shed more tears that night than the rest of the week combined. So many people from so many phases of our life were there. Aleta remarked to me, "It's like a really sad wedding." But it was truly interesting to see how our reactions changed from person to person. The Savior said we are to "mourn with those that mourn; yea, and comfort those that stand in need of comfort" (Mosiah 18:9), and I saw it happen before my eyes. As people came to us, nervous and unsure of what to say, we cracked a joke to ease the tension and gave them a smile. To those who had been heartbroken by the loss, we gave them a simple embrace. To those who had been agonizing about their own trial or thinking of their own children of a similar age, we offered words of comfort. To those too sad to speak, we simply cried. In the end, *we* were able to comfort others, even though they had come to comfort us. This was a blessing I did not expect.

16

The Funeral

The morning of the funeral we quietly got ready and made our way to our old church building. When we arrived, the funeral home had already moved Holland's casket into place and had begun setting up the flowers. We greeted the family that came early to help set up and visited briefly with one of the members of the Seventy who had blessed Holland in the hospital and his wife. We were grateful that he had agreed to speak and preside over the funeral. Since we had kept in contact with him through email, this was a friendly reunion.

Before too many people arrived, I sat in the back of the cultural hall and looked over my notes for the eulogy I had prepared. I gave a silent prayer and was briefly visited by Holland, who told me again of the peace and love that she was receiving from the Savior. She was allowed to witness the funeral and would be present to hear all the remarks. Holland reminded me of her love for me and that she didn't want me to be sad. This brief encounter took away any nervousness I had and filled me with the peace that everything said would be according to the Lord's will.

We had a short viewing before the funeral and then we gathered for the family prayer. We wanted it to be set up like her bedtime routine, so I read one of her favorite stories, the last story I ever read to her, *You Are Special*, by Max Lucado. Then we tucked her in with her favorite blankets, handed her fluffy monkey to Dallin for him to remember her by, and then stood by as they closed the casket. Aleta's dad offered a sincere family prayer that brought the peace that we needed in order to start the service.

We then made our way down the hall to the chapel. I kissed Aleta as I left to take my place on the stand with the other speakers while our friend played Holland's favorite hymns and Primary songs on the organ. Looking out over the crowd that spread to the third overflow, I realized there were five to seven hundred people present. I couldn't believe how many people had shown up: most of my coworkers, members of our old and new wards, kids from the singles ward I served in, Holland's friends, and, of course, most of our family. I was surprised to see some of the kids from the Latinos in Action group that had hosted the 5K.

Our former bishop stood to begin the services, and Aleta's sister gave the opening prayer. My mom was the first speaker and gave a life sketch of Holland, describing all of Holland's birthdays and Halloweens. We laughed at the stories she shared (even if she did fudge on many details in the way only my mom could). It touched my heart when she mentioned that she had given Holland a kiss when she was born and another little kiss when she died. Like my mom herself, her talk was fun, honest, spiritual, but most of all, sincere.

My niece was the next speaker—she had been Holland's primary babysitter for years. She listed off all of the things that Holland loved—a long list, because Holland loved everything. My niece's words, each said through a steady stream of tears, were exactly what I needed to hear, and they reminded me of everything I loved about my little girl. Then my dear friend and his daughter sang a beautiful rendition of "Paradise" by Coldplay. It had always been one of Holland's favorite songs, and as we heard the words again, they seemed to perfectly describe exactly what she had been through and where she now was. "And so lying underneath those stormy skies, she'd say, 'Oh, . . . I know the sun must set to rise.' This could be paradise."[1]

Next, it was my chance to speak, and as usual, my talk was long. We recorded the funeral,[2] and each time I listen to the talk I gave, I want to take notes—the words were not my own. I know the words I spoke that day were from the Spirit because they were exactly what I needed to hear. I only hope they spoke a similar peace to all those who were there. The talk is best summed up in this line: "If you remember Holland and you don't remember Christ, you are doing her memory an injustice. I don't say this to be cruel—I say this because it's truth." Everything that little girl was (and is now) was because of and through Christ.

I also shared the lessons I learned from Holland by looking back on her life. Often the last chapter of a book or the last episode of a TV series helps you to see the meaning of the whole picture. Similarly, as I looked back at all of the chapters of Holland's life, I was able to see greater meaning in these lessons she taught me.

1. Face the future with faith. I thought about the quote from Elder Holland that had inspired us in naming Holland. Elder Holland said, "Faith is for the future. Faith builds on the past but never longs to stay there. Faith trusts that God has great things in store for each of us and that Christ truly is the 'high priest of good things to come.'"[3] This lesson was taught to me at her birth and at her death.

2. Exceed expectations. Holland was always ahead of the curve. She grew quickly physically, emotionally, socially, and spiritually. Whenever she went into a surgery, she always bounced back better and faster than the doctors anticipated she would. She was not content with simply meeting expectations. Because Holland didn't have much time, she always went above and beyond what was expected of her.

3. Make the most of each moment. She had an old soul and knew that she didn't have much time to accomplish what she was here to do. She touched more lives in four years than most do in their entire adult lives. Especially in the last fourteen months of her life, she drew many people closer to Christ.

4. Be brave in the face of adversity. She bravely endured seven surgeries and multiple chemo treatments and blood draws. But the real bravery I needed was in the eternal perspective of the gospel. Christ overcame death and sin for us, and with those conquered, what is left to fear? With that mind-set I was able to overcome doubt and fear and find peace and comfort in times of life's greatest trials.

I prayed that the words I spoke would inspire all those who were there, and I believed that they did. Interestingly, many people told me that my words inspired them and increased their faith—but it was their faith and prayers that were sustaining me at that very moment. Faith is very reciprocal that way: as we exercise faith, it grows stronger in us, and as we give faith to others, we gain faith in ourselves. The words I spoke on that day were spoken more by the Spirit than my physical mouth. And I also believe that my talk was, in many ways, Holland's way to speak to all of her friends and family as well.

After my talk, the children sang Holland's favorite Primary song, "Holding Hands Around the World." One little kid sang really loudly and off-key the whole time, and it was great because it was just like Holland was in there singing with them. Then the bishop said some beautiful words in his quiet humble way, and it was clear that Holland had sincerely impacted his life.

And finally, our friend, the member of the Seventy, spoke. He invited me to leave the stand and sit next to Aleta in the congregation—"Because the only way you'll get through this is together." He had written us a letter, detailing five things he wanted to make sure we knew:

1. It is not your fault Holland was called home.
2. Holland's spirit is not a four-year-old spirit; it is a mature spirit.
3. Holland does not want you to mourn for her.
4. Your perspective on life will expand.
5. Be happy and righteous in your roles as mother and father to the rest of your family.

Chapter 16

These were especially meaningful since I knew that he had lost a young child as well. At the time, these were valuable pieces of advice, and I now hold these things as some of the very pillars of my testimony. I was very glad that he agreed to speak and to preside, since his words were very inspired and needed.

To close, we sang "God Be with You Till We Meet Again," and my sister said the closing prayer. Holland's pallbearers were the same priesthood holders who held her in her baby blessing circle—mainly her uncles and cousins. We made our way through the crowd to the parking lot and then drove the short drive to the cemetery next to our old house. Somehow it seemed fitting that we would be able to see our old house from where Holland was buried. Being in that cemetery reminded me of "Happy Holland's Day," when Holland wanted to see the Memorial Day flowers here. We gathered around her grave, and my father said the very somber and spiritual gravesite dedication. Before we left the cemetery, we filled up yellow balloons and all wrote messages on them and let them float up to her. On my balloon, I wrote "You and I always loved scary stuff, but now there is no more scary stuff. I will always love you, Daddy."

Although we had not been members of our new ward for very long, they offered to provide the family luncheon. They did a great job—each table had a centerpiece made up of Holland's favorite toys. And they served Holland's favorite foods: chicken nuggets, fries, and macaroni and cheese. After we ate, I performed a song I wrote for Holland.[4] We then had a family testimony meeting where everyone wrote down their favorite Holland memories on index cards. It was a tender experience of family bonding and spiritual strength.

It was a long, exhausting day, but the Spirit and Holland's presence had sustained us. As I struggled to fall asleep that night, I was blown away by the overwhelming support that Holland had received in this life and the love that she was receiving in the next life.

The next day we went to church, but after sacrament meeting I just felt like garbage. I couldn't understand—all week I had been sustained and strengthened, but now I felt depressed and grief-stricken. When I got home, I realized that many of the people who had attended the funeral thought that we appeared to be doing so well that they had stopped praying for us. I could feel the lack of prayers that had once been sustaining us. I could also feel that after the funeral, Holland was no longer with us. She had fully gone on to start her great work that she had ahead of her.

Notes

1. Coldplay, "Paradise," written by William Champion, Christopher Anthony John Martin, Jonathan Mark Buckland, Brian Eno, and Guy Rupert Berryman (Peermusic Publishing and Universal Music Publishing Group, 2011).
2. "Bryan's Talk at Holland's Funeral," YouTube video, 31:01, the eulogy given at Holland Young's funeral on August 10, 2013, posted by Bryan Young, May 30, 2014, www.youtube.com/watch?v=V0DOE6toHDg.
3. Jeffrey R. Holland, "Remember Lot's Wife: Faith Is for the Future" (Brigham Young University devotional, January 13, 2009), speeches.byu.edu.
4. "The Son Is Coming Up," YouTube video, 4:13, a song about Holland's battle with brain tumors, posted by Bryan Young, July 17, 2013, www.youtube.com/watch?v=Z6du1X6ieY0.

17

Moving Forward

In the days after the funeral, many family members remained in town, and Aleta's parents stayed with us. As I said before, I could feel the power of prayer that left us at this time and I could feel that Holland's spirit had moved on. It was clear that we would need the power of family to move forward. If we were going to pick up the pieces, we would need to rely on each other. Aleta and I would need to be the strength for each other, and we would also need our close friends and family to lift and guide us during this time.

Before everyone went home, we had a big family BBQ up Provo Canyon with my family and Aleta's family. This was a fun opportunity to just enjoy our family again. The fun and conversations that we had that day showed us that our extended family would continue to be there to lighten our burdens and give us the love and support we would need. It was hard to watch Holland's cousins play and have fun, realizing that she would no longer be a part of those games. But comfort came from knowing that she was engaged in something greater now. As weeks went by, I also found comfort in helping our extended family go through their own individual grieving processes just as I was going through mine. I was grateful for the eternal vision that I had been given of God's plan for Holland, and I reminded my family of it as well.

Meant for Heaven

A week after the funeral, I went back to work at the Provo School District. This was hard but it was also nice to be back in old routines. Work gave my mind something else to focus on. Many of my coworkers were cautious in how they approached me, but the fact that many of them were psychologists helped. Over those next few weeks and months, I had countless conversations that always led back to the gospel and how the Lord had guided us and comforted us through this situation. I got to watch the plan unfold that we had set up before this life. Each one of these individual conversations was helping my coworkers draw closer to God and helping them through their own situations. I had been assigned to two new schools that year and so I had many conversations with teachers who had no idea who I was and what I had just been through. This helped me to be more comfortable sharing our story with strangers and took away a lot of the awkwardness of answering questions like, "How many kids do you have?"

As helpful as going back to work was for me, it was harder for Aleta. We had just moved into this much bigger house, which now felt like some kind of silent mausoleum. It was so spacious and quiet. The house that we had bought to fill with our young expanding family now seemed way too big and way too empty. Aleta was left in this quiet house alone with Dallin, who hardly talked yet. Because we had just moved, we didn't really have any friends in our new neighborhood to help her with that transition. But I think this helped Aleta to draw closer to Dallin and to Holland's spirit. And in a way, the new house helped because it was not full of painful memories of Holland—she had only lived there for two weeks and we had cleaned out most of her stuff the week of the funeral. It was a new house to start new memories in. Dallin was just beginning to walk and talk but we missed the sounds of childish play and the constant chatter of a four-year-old. I remember turning on some of Holland's favorite cartoons just so it could sound like a kid still lived there. In that silence was a lot of tears and painful conversations between Aleta and me about what life would be like now without Holland. We would often talk about her and what she was doing now and what she would have been doing if she were still here.

We were pained as we watched other children starting pre-school and kindergarten, knowing that Holland would never go to school as she had always wanted. When we went to the movies, we were sad that she would never watch them. When we saw her friends playing, we thought of the games she would never play. There was pain in the thoughts of the milestones we would not see in this life: school, baptism, mission, wedding, and all the things you look forward to as a young parent. Though we were haunted by what she would never do in this life, we found joy in what she did do and what she was now capable of doing. We found peace in the work that she was now doing for the Lord, that her real mission was now being fulfilled. There was also a sense of joy and relief that she was no longer in pain. It had been hard to watch her deteriorate and not be able to do all she wanted to, and now she was not limited by disease and fatigue. When we thought back to all of her fun memories, they made us smile and laugh, but they would also bring tears to our eyes as we thought about not being able to create new memories anymore. We knew though that this was God's will for her, and that often took away the sting of those moments and conversations.

Many times as Aleta and I sat on the couch, talking about Holland, we would both be able to feel her presence in the room. It was hard to describe, but it was clear she was there to comfort us in times of need. We could almost point to where she was in the room, but we could not see her or touch her. As time has passed, these events have decreased in frequency, but we continue to find ways to feel her with us. We have been amazed at the times that we have been doing something as a family that she would have loved and then we get in the car and the first song that comes on the radio is "Paradise" by Coldplay or "Trouble" by Taylor Swift. As these songs have become less and less popular, it becomes more and more miraculous every time they find a way to sneak into our family moments. They always bring smiles to our faces or tears to our eyes, depending on the moment.

Holland's Friends

Holland's friends dealt with her death in different ways. Because we had just moved, she had already said good-bye to many of her friends from our old neighborhood and church. It was clear that many of her friends' parents had had to sit down and have hard discussions with their small children about death. When we would run into the families of her friends, their reactions were always so interesting. Some were sad, some were happy to see us, and some were just confused. I remember running into one of her friends at a baby blessing a few months after the funeral, and she looked at us so confused and said, "You're Holland's dad. Holland's dead. What are you doing here?" In her mind, it was as if we had stopped existing when Holland had. Another friend of hers came up to me and said, "Holland died and that's sad, but she's going to be resurrected and that's happy. I hope she is resurrected in time to come to my birthday party!" It was obvious that her parents had had a lesson about death with her, but I informed them they might need another one to clear that up with her.

Holland's best friend was Alice. She was about a year and a half older than Holland but they loved playing with each other. Aleta worked with Alice's mom at church, and they are very close friends as well. Watching Alice grieve has been the most informative to me, because she has seemed to continue a spiritual relationship with Holland, more so than her other friends. She used to draw pictures for Holland and want to bring them to us. She still lives by the cemetery where Holland is buried and will ask to go visit Holland from time to time. Every time we see their family, her face lights up to see us, because she is reminded of her friend Holland. After Holland died, we gave Alice Holland's ladybug pillow pet. She would often show it to people and explain that this was a gift from her friend Holland who had died. She truly treasured it as we hoped she would. Not long after Holland died, Alice's dad was diagnosed with colon cancer, and I think that was extra hard for Alice because she had watched Holland suffer through similar things. After witnessing Holland's experience, I think their entire family feared this would be a death sentence for him as it was for her. Luckily, he bravely fought his cancer and is now in remission. I know that Holland helped their family go through that experience with courage and comfort.

Alice was recently baptized, which was a very emotional moment for our family. When we were invited I knew that we would feel Holland's spirit there during her friend's sacred moment, and we did. I was invited to be a part of the circle when Alice received the gift of the Holy Ghost. Tears streamed down my face as her father spoke because I knew that this gift would allow Holland to better communicate with her friend and help her as she continued to grow. I knew that often when Alice would hear a still, small voice keeping her from danger or guiding her toward success, that voice would be Holland's.

Watching Dallin deal with the death of Holland has been interesting. He had just turned one year old when Holland died, so he couldn't really communicate his sorrow and grief. Often he would just crawl around looking for her. But his biggest grief was seen in the car. He would look over at her car seat and wonder where that kid who used to talk so much had gone. After we removed her car seat, he would still longingly look over at where she had been. Especially when he was little, there were moments when we knew that she visited him—times when we could hear him laughing in his bed at night or staring at a spot in the room so intently you knew he saw something we didn't. Dallin is now four years old and is very aware of Holland's presence in our family. He talks about his sister who lives with Jesus. Often after family home evening lessons he will talk about Jesus dying and being resurrected so that Holland can also be resurrected. The concept of death is hard for small children, but he certainly understands that he has a family member who is with him even though he can't see her.

Dallin has grown to be so much like Holland in so many ways. He physically looks a lot like her, his voice often sounds like hers, and his mannerisms resemble hers. When he gets excited, he will jump up and down with a wide-open mouth, and it's like seeing her again. Granted he is his own kid too—he is more shy and reserved and sensitive than she was. I often think there is no way he could handle everything that she went through just because his temperament is so mild. He is now the same age that Holland was when she started the chemo. I watch him accomplish and learn things and do things without the limitations that bound Holland, and I wonder what she would have been capable of if she had never gotten sick.

We are quickly approaching the time when Dallin will be older than Holland was when she died. I know it will be hard to watch him hit milestones that she never reached, but it helps because I don't think of her stuck as a four-year-old; I think of her as an adult now. I have such an adult relationship with her in the spirit that I don't mourn for her four-year-old self anymore.

18

Holland in the Temple

After the funeral, I held Holland to her word that if I wanted to be with her I would need to go to the temple, not her gravesite. I still visit her gravesite, but that is when I miss her body, because that is all that is there. But when I go to the temple, I am able to be in her presence and hear her voice. I am able to visit her spirit in all its purity.

The week after Holland's funeral, before I went back to work, Aleta and I decided to return to the temple for the first time since the day Holland died. Once we were in the celestial room, we sat and bowed our heads in prayer. We could both feel Holland's spirit with us. I heard her voice in my mind, and she began to instruct me on the work she was doing. Holland told me she was teaching our family members who had never had the gospel in mortality. She talked about her uncle, Aleta's brother who had passed away fifteen years earlier. His work was to help spirits transition after mortality to their new spiritual state. She told me about the role that I would play in helping in this work. She said, "I will teach these spirits, Grandpa [my father who is very involved in genealogy work] will find them, and you will do their work in the temple."

After we opened our tear-filled eyes from our silent prayers, Aleta and I were asked by a temple worker if we had time to help with proxy sealing ordinances. We had never been asked to leave the celestial room to help with sealings before, but we took this as an invitation from Holland and gladly accepted. As we sat across the altar from each other as we had on the day we were married, we were reminded of the sacred covenants we had made together. We were reminded that when Holland was born she became a part of that covenant as well. She would receive these same blessings of eternal life and exaltation that we would receive. The Spirit reminded us of the blessings of resurrection that would be fulfilled when Christ returns to the earth. Though Holland's body was now separated from us, her spirit was sealed to us for as long as we kept our promises to the Lord. We were reminded that in a future day we would all be reunited and resurrected as a family. Most of all, we rejoiced in the blessings of eternity, the fact that our family would not cease at death but would continue on forever.

I left the temple knowing that Holland was with us going forward. I knew I would not only see her again with the resurrection, but if I continued to attend the temple, I could develop a relationship with her as a spirit. I vowed to strive to attend the temple as often as I could and set up my schedule so that I could go early on Monday mornings every week before work. Because I could feel her spirit inside the temple, I knew I needed to be there. Working with my dad, I had a consistent stream of names of deceased family members to take to the temple so that we could both fulfill Holland's wish of getting these people the ordinances of salvation.

After a few weeks, I was amazed at how Holland appeared to be growing in her maturity as a spirit. Though she had only been out of this world for a few weeks, she would now be teaching, leading, guiding, and watching over our family and me. Our roles were being reversed—she was now the one teaching me about Jesus and His gospel. After a few weeks of regular temple attendance, I was disheartened to find that I couldn't feel Holland's spirit, even in the temple. I was upset—I thought this was part of the deal, that if I went to the temple I would be able to communicate with her. But the Lord told me that, unlike the Holy Ghost, Holland was a finite spirit. She could only be in one place at a time. She had other work to do and she was not available to be at my beck and call every time I went to the temple. My relationship with her was much like a father with a grown adult daughter. Sometimes when you call to just say hi, she is at work or school and can't talk. So you leave a message and know that she'll get back to you when she can.

A month after Holland died, I had another profound experience in the temple. Before work I went to the temple and Holland said to me, "I'm here with my sister and she really wants to come down and be a part of our family!" I was a bit taken back by this, since Dallin was only thirteen months old, we had just lost Holland, and we were not that interested in trying to replace her. I responded that we decided we would try in a year or so to have another kid. "No," Holland said, "She wants to come down and you need to talk to Mom about this." So when I got home I told Aleta about what Holland had said, knowing she would not be a fan of this idea. Aleta informed me that she was a day late on her period, and after a pregnancy test, we discovered that, sure enough, she was already pregnant. Long story short, it turned out that this baby was not the sister we had planned on. This was our son, Nelson Davis Young, born almost nine months to the day after Holland died. I figured Nelson and Holland had passed on their way to and from this earth and probably didn't have much of an opportunity to talk. But I know that they knew each other before this life and they know each other now.

It was two years later that this little sister, Hinckley Jane Young, was born. Watching this little baby, I know that she knew Holland before this life and currently interacts with her. She will smile and stare at the wall, and I can feel Holland's spirit near. Hinckley has even started mimicking that same wide smile that was so characteristic of Holland. In the time leading up to Hinckley's birth, I would hear Holland talk about her, how excited she was to come down and be a part of our family, to get a body and to bring souls closer to Christ. However, the spirit

of my unborn daughter often communicated with me the concerns and apprehensions she had about the state of the world at this time. She wanted to come down but was fearful of the hate and evil in the world and the hardships that were ahead for our family and the world. In one such moment I communicated to this pre-earth spirit that if she was coming to *this* family, she didn't need to be afraid of the world because I would make sure that this family always followed the will of the Lord and if we did that there was nothing to be afraid of. Now I look down at this innocent peaceful baby and know that her spirit knows that I will always trust in the Lord and she feels the peace of that commitment still today.

I continued to receive communication from Holland about her work and the role that she was playing in my life. I also began to see the power that sharing her story would bring. On one occasion, right after the school year, Holland directed me to help someone in the temple. I was doing a session mid-day, and I noticed a lady who also worked for the Provo School District. I didn't know her name or really what she did—I had just seen her around some of the schools. Throughout the session I felt that Holland wanted me to share with her my story. I thought that odd and hesitated, since I had never really talked to this lady

Chapter 18

before. Once I got into the celestial room, I decided to wait for her to come in and if she sat down I would talk to her. Unfortunately she immediately left the celestial room without sitting down. As she was obviously in a hurry, I brushed off the prompting to talk to her. But Holland insisted, so I ran her down and didn't catch up to her until she was downstairs. I stopped her and she seemed somewhat caught off guard.

I told her, "This may sound weird since I don't really know you; I work with you but I don't even know your name. But I feel prompted to tell you about my daughter who died of cancer last year." I proceeded to detail all that Holland had been through and how I had known her cancer was part of the plan we had set up before this life to help people draw closer to Christ. I went on for several minutes before I even let her talk. When I eventually stopped to let her respond, she told me her name was Susan and that she worked with blind students in the school district. Then, with tears streaming down her face, she told me that she was just beginning her second round of chemo treatments for breast cancer. The first time had been very spiritual for her and she had drawn closer to the Lord, but when it came back she was bitter and upset and felt that God no longer cared about her. She had come to the temple that day to see if she could even feel the Spirit anymore. But throughout the whole session she just felt angry and upset and didn't even want to stay in the celestial room. She had concluded that God didn't care about her anymore. But then I stopped her and told her Holland's story, about the many times her own tumors returned and how God was always with us. It was clear to both of us that God had sent me to talk with her.

We continued to talk about her life experiences and all the lessons that we had each learned from our journeys through cancer. We then wished each other well and went our separate ways, but as I went to my car in the parking lot, her car was parked next to mine. So we continued to talk about the Lord's love for each of us. She detailed some additional trials that she had faced in her love life and I told her of some of my experiences in the singles ward I had served in. We both left forever changed by the interaction. She left knowing that God had not forgotten about her. I left knowing what it felt like to be a tool in the Lord's hands and how much Holland's story could help even complete strangers. I have not seen her since, and I don't know how her journey progresses. But I know that God and Holland wanted me to help her that day.

Frequent temple visits made for many sacred moments with Holland, such as her cousin's wedding, learning of Holland's relationship with the Savior, or finding out about our upcoming baby girl. However, one of the most sacred temple revelations came when Holland told me she had been authorized to show me the moment of her resurrection. It humbled me to the core and affected me so much I found it hard to walk afterward.

Though this is one of the more special and sacred moments for my family and me, I feel it is important to share because it will hopefully instill in each person who reads this book the reality and importance of the resurrection. We will all face death in our lifetime but we can also look forward to the glorious day of resurrection. Our pains and sorrows and physical separations are only for a brief moment in the eternities. We can all look forward to the moment of reunion in the spirit and flesh. For each person we have lost, we will find them again.

In this vision, we were outside because I remember green grass, but it was bright, very bright. Looking back, it must have been at the cemetery where she is buried because I could see the mountains in the background. Holland was small and dressed in white, similar to how she was buried. But her hair was full and long, past her shoulders, with a slight curl to it. She ran to me and I quickly embraced her, and her skin was so soft and much more full and colorful than it was in this life. We both shed tears as I took her by the hand and led her to Aleta, who also embraced her. Meanwhile, Dallin, who appeared to be in early adolescence, somewhere between nine and thirteen, stood behind her, and Nelson, who was slightly smaller, stood beside Dallin. I remember other family members being there but not clearly enough to recollect their appearance. Though the vision was simple, the emotions and feelings of that moment were impressed on my soul and will stay with me until that moment arrives. Holland made clear that this moment will only happen if we stay worthy and choose to keep our faith in the Lord.

Holland's Role in the Last Days

As I attended the temple, Holland also taught me more about her work on the other side of the veil. From what she said, the work in the next life was changing. Instead of focusing on the dead, they were working with the living to prepare them for what was coming, to prepare the earth for the Second Coming of Jesus Christ. The spirits on the other side were now mainly working to prepare and strengthen their loved ones and family members for the trials that were to precede His earthly return.

Since that time, I have felt her presence with me more often. I have called on her to help her brothers when they were sick or scared. I have seen her influence help us as a family by prompting us to get more food storage, emergency supplies, and extra clothing for the boys. She has guided not only our physical preparedness but also our spiritual preparedness. We have learned to trust in the Lord more, pray more, love the scriptures more, and more fully apply conference talks to our lives. We have begun to speak in a way that has helped those around us to feel the same sense of urgency.

The truth is that each of us has family on the other side urging us to do the same thing: prepare for the coming of the Lord. Each name we take to the temple, each loved one we tragically lose on this earth is another angel authorized to help us in our cause of righteousness. As we strive to build Zion, we do so with the help of our departed family and loved ones. The kingdom of God is not of this world and neither are its occupants.

It is also important to note that we consist of a physical body and a spiritual body. Though our loved ones may be separated from their physical bodies, they are very much alive in spiritual form. And as we enliven the senses of our spiritual bodies, we will learn how to feel their presence and communicate with them. So often after the death of a loved one we strive to see them again, to hear their voice, to touch their skin, to smell their scent, to say one last, "I love you," or to give one last kiss. In short, we try to make them physical again so that we can communicate with them physically. But the answer is not in changing them—it's in changing us. As we strengthen our spiritual senses, we can begin to interact with these loved ones spiritually, since our spiritual bodies and their spiritual bodies are still very much intact.

The idea of spiritual communication is very hard for some people to understand. I will attempt to try and explain it using a couple metaphors. Imagine if we kept our eyes closed for twenty years or so. We would find that when we opened them we would not be able to see as we once did. Our eyes would be weakened to the point that it would make it hard to trust the things we saw. The same is true of our spirits. If we have spent a lifetime denying our spiritual senses, then how can we be expected to trust the feelings and promptings that can only be explained by the Spirit?

There are angels all around us—they are constantly guiding, prompting, pushing, and moving us, but we refuse to, or sometimes are unable to, trust our spiritual senses enough to know that. After decades of neglect, our spiritual abilities can become atrophied. Much like when we start to exercise for the first time, we begin to push the limits of our weakened muscles and they become stronger and can be trusted and pushed more and more. Similarly, as we trust in our spiritual senses, we can recognize these spiritual beings that are all around us. We will find not only that we begin to recognize their presence, but that we can become spiritually stronger ourselves and have more spiritual promptings. We can grow to the point that we trust our spiritual senses more than our physical ones.

If you want to know how you will have the strength to face the challenges that are ahead of you, the prophesied calamities that will rival none in the history of this world, you must begin to recognize and strengthen your spiritual communication and senses. Think of a detective who has trained her eyes and perceptions to find clues in a crime scene. When a new crime scene presents itself she relies on the skills gained in the previous case. The same is true of us: if we want to be able to call on the power of angels to minister unto us in times of great trial, we must begin now by calling on them in the face of daily adversity. As we do so, we will find that we are spiritually strong enough to trust in the guidance of these loved ones when they are authorized by the Lord to assist us.

In order to grow my spiritual gifts, I must do the same thing—seek to use my gifts not for my own desires but for God's. If I seek to spiritually see Holland, then I need to seek her because then I can help to build the kingdom of God even more, not because she's my daughter and I miss her. By seeing her spiritually, I can then see the spiritual world around me and help others to do the same. And when we all have gained and magnified our abilities, we can build Zion, a people of one heart and one mind, which is God's heart and his mind. We must seek after Zion, not because of the peace that it will bring us, but for the peace it will bring the world.

We must be willing to sacrifice our peace and comfort so that the world may gain it. As we use our spiritual gifts and all that the Lord has given us to build this kingdom, we become joint heirs with Christ because we have sacrificed our desires and wills to build up our brothers and sisters. We can start this process in our marriages and families by giving all that we have to our spouse and children—not because it makes us feel good, but because it makes them feel good. As we serve and strive together, we become greater than we were and we build each other up and become of one heart and one mind. And as we put aside our desires and unite our will with Christ's, we become one and we will be called Zion.

Epilogue

Three Years Later

As I finish this book that has been over three years in the making, I have been able to look back on the roller coaster of Holland's battle with cancer and see the good with the bad. Although at times I just wanted to get off the ride, I can now say with all surety that I am better for having taken it. I am a better man today than I was before Holland got sick. I am a better man today than I was the day Holland died. I am no longer on this roller coaster. For lack of a better phrase, I am now on a "stairway to heaven." Each step brings me closer to God, closer to my family, closer to Holland.

Looking back at the last three years, I can see how I have become a better husband, father, priesthood holder, employee, friend, neighbor, and son of God. I have said many times that I would not wish this journey on anyone, but if you are going to take it, do it right. Do not become bitter and broken down by the trials of your life. Instead, allow them to build you up into a new and refined spiritual being. Put aside your selfish desires and focus on the things that make you more than your natural self and more of the divine spirit within you.

Over the years, many people have told me that Holland's story has been an inspiration to them in one way or another. Some have told me that her story has helped them believe in God

Epilogue

again, helped them save their marriage or get out of a marriage that was destructive, inspired them to go to the temple or on missions, helped them magnify their callings, get new jobs, lose weight, love their kids more, love their spouse more, become more Christlike, put their own trials into perspective or overcome them, put their trust in the Lord, overcome temptation, and be better overall. If Holland has helped you do any of these things, I'm glad. That means she has fulfilled her mission of bringing souls to Christ.

A couple years ago I was giving a lesson about Holland and the plan of salvation to a group of seminary students at the state mental hospital where I worked. One of the kids was a bit of a punk and would try to antagonize others, and as I told my story, he raised his hand and said, "This is a bunch of garbage! If God really loved you, He wouldn't have let your daughter die!"

I stopped, looked him in the eye, and said, "If you have felt any closer to God while I have been talking about this; if you believe any principle of her story; if it has helped you draw closer to God, then I'm glad she died. Because I would rather her die and return to the Lord than have her live and you not return to Him."

And the same is true of you. I don't necessarily know who you are or why you felt compelled to read this whole story, but if you did, I thank you. I wrote this story because the Lord told me it could help people, and if this story has helped you in any way, I am glad. If you have felt the Spirit at any time while reading this and it prompted you to do something different in your life, I beg you to do it. You will be better for it. As you read, if you felt love, hope, kindness, or warmth, that may have been Holland telling you that this story is true. She could be with you right now as you read these words. And I hope that you will make the most of her sacrifice for you. Before this life even started, she was willing to give up her young life so that you could draw closer to the Lord. Trust in the Lord and draw nearer to Him and He will love you and support you through every trial this life has to offer. This is my testimony and I know it by the power of the Holy Ghost and

Epilogue

through all the experiences that you have just read and more. Jesus Christ is my Friend, my Brother, my Savior, my King, the Author and Finisher of my faith. I love Him with all my heart as I love my little girl with all my heart. They are both real and continue to be an active part of my life.

Appendix A

Community Rallies to Pay for Child's Five Brain Surgeries

Rena Lesue-Smithey

In the last seven months, three-year-old Holland Young has endured five brain surgeries to remove tumors, and after the latest procedure her family is waiting to hear whether the growths are benign—as doctors originally thought—or if she'll have to start chemotherapy.

Even though the family is insured, the out-of-pocket costs for the unexpected medical bills have wiped out their savings. In addition, Holland's mom had a baby this year.

With the help of the community and a website called give-forward.com, the Provo family hopes to raise six thousand dollars to pay medical bills. This is their second effort with the site to raise the money, as they didn't reach their fund-raising goal for the third and fourth surgeries. And Spanish Fork High School's Latinos in Action group is hosting a 5K run in support of Holland in March. All proceeds will go to the Young family's medical fund to pay for Holland's surgeries.

"Holland started having headaches around her birthday in May," Holland's mother, Aleta, said. "She complained that her head hurt, and it was waking her up at night."

Aleta explained that the first time Holland threw up, she wondered if she caught a virus. Holland continued to sleep poorly, and threw up again days later, but she never had a fever.

Appendix A

By the second week, Holland was vomiting every other day, and always in the morning. They took her to a clinic where a pediatrician told them to leave for Primary Children's Medical Center immediately. The next day, Holland had her first brain surgery.

Doctors had found a golf ball-sized tumor on Holland's cerebellum. She had two brain surgeries in June and two more in August. After the fourth, the family was relieved when Holland was given a clean bill of health, but early this month, Holland began to experience nausea and vomiting again, signs that the tumor had returned. Doctors found two tumors and a cyst the size of a small orange. She had her fifth surgery on December 10.

"It was disappointing when we found out about the regrowth two weeks ago," Aleta said. "We thought we were all done in August. The MRI was all clear. There was nothing left."

After her fourth surgery, little Holland also was excited to be finished with hospitals.

"No more doctors. No more hospitals," Aleta said Holland told her. "They got all the bad stuff out."

For the second time, Aleta's sister-in-law, Jamie Marshall, set up the donation site after several people mentioned that they wanted to offer financial support. Marshall titled the site, "Holland, Our Little Fighter" because of Holland's strength in adversity.

"Once you meet Holland, it's hard not to love her spirit and spunk. She's energetic, happy, and always having fun," family friend Nancy Miramontes said. "This little girl is a true fighter. Even after such invasive procedures, Holland remains undefeated. She's done her part and now we need to do ours. Holland is a reminder that nothing is impossible and we just want her to know that we are here to fight right alongside her."

People have been helping the Youngs in other ways as well. "We've had a lot of presents, stuffed animals, balloons, meals provided, and donations," Aleta said. "Bryan (Aleta's husband) and I have been so grateful. Pretty much our entire savings, which we were going to use for a house, was used to pay for the first couple of surgeries."

Appendix A

Miramontes explained that help is coming from a variety of sources.

"Family members, ward members, the school psychology cohort, and friends have joined together to cover things like meals and Christmas presents for the family," said Miramontes, a school psychologist and Latinos in Action adviser at Spanish Fork High, who met Bryan Young at Brigham Young University when they were in the same school psychology program. "I think what the Young family will need in the upcoming months is financial assistance to pay for these five brain surgeries. The family's life savings have been wiped out while trying to cover the expenses, and Holland's journey is not over yet."

Doctors have told Aleta that she'd need to take Holland in for an MRI every six months for the next several years to check on her progress, and then once a year for two years after that.

Bryan and Aleta Young have another child, Dallin, who was born this year during the family's crisis with Holland.

"The Youngs are the most caring and positive family I know. Throughout this entire ordeal, the family has never lost hope or complained about anything. Their Facebook updates are always positive and uplifting. Even when they've had to communicate bad news, it's always been followed by gratitude for all those who have prayed for them. All the family has ever asked for is prayers," Miramontes said.

If she could swap places with her daughter, Aleta would, she said.

"Holland doesn't understand why she's getting poked in the arm by doctors and nurses. It's hard to reason with a three-year-old, but she's been very brave," said Aleta. "You never really expect your kid to have a brain tumor."

To help Holland and the Youngs, visit the donation site at www.giveforward.com/hollandourlittlefighter.

Rena Lesue-Smithey, "Community Rallies to Pay for Child's Five Brain Surgeries," *Daily Herald*, December 19, 2012, www.heraldextra.com.

Appendix B

12 Days of Miracles:
Day 12 Holland's Miracle—How a Cyst
Turned into a Miracle

The Young family thought they were in the clear after their daughter Holland's last brain surgery in August. Holland was diagnosed with juvenile pilocytic astrocytoma (JPA)—a benign, slow-growing tumor in her brain. She had to have four surgeries to completely remove the tumor.

Holland started having headaches again this December. A scan revealed a cyst had grown in her brain, and a subsequent brain surgery was required. Given the time of year, and all the previous surgeries, Bryan and his wife, Aleta, were worried and frustrated. Little did they know, this cyst was a miracle in disguise.

After the surgery, doctors found that Holland had a more serious condition known as pilomyxoid astrocytoma—a more aggressive brain tumor, with the potential for other serious complications. Holland's next MRI wasn't scheduled until March, so if it hadn't been detected early, it could have continued to grow and caused other complications. Fortunately, doctors were able to remove the tumor and begin treatments.

Having had five brain surgeries this year, it is miraculous that Holland has not had any skill loss or change in personality. She has bounced back from each surgery, and kept her bubbly, energetic zest for life.

Appendix B

The events of this year haven't been easy on the Young family. In addition to Holland's medical problems, they welcomed a new baby boy, Dallin, to their family. They made it through all the difficulties because of their faith, family, and church support. Their optimism has also been a crucial component.

Holland never walks. She runs everywhere—no matter the circumstances. She loves living and is excited by almost everything. She always has a grin on her face. She is crazy about BYU football and especially Cosmo. She tells jokes and loves to get other people laughing. One of her favorite things is cartoons, but don't ask which her favorite is. It will probably change in a few weeks.

"12 Days of Miracles: Day 12 Holland's Miracle—How a Cyst Turned into a Miracle," December 25, 2012, www.primarychildrenshospitalblog .org/?s=2012.

Appendix C

Holland Young's Battle

Alexis Kaufusi

Yesterday my mother, Michelle, texted me, telling me she had an idea and needed my opinion. Naturally I called her, wondering what she would possibly want my opinion about, and she said that there was a little girl who was three. Her name was Holland. She's from Provo and from an avid BYU family, and she had multiple brain tumors. Immediately I felt as if my heart weighed twenty pounds as it sunk into my chest. I then told Chelle we needed to do what we could to help this little girl and her family out, just like all of you helped me out.

** Fast-forward twenty-four hours **

As we approached the home where Holland Young lives, I couldn't help but be so nervous. Out front was a metal yard decoration sporting the BYU logo, but then my attention was directed to the squealing giggles of a little girl as the front door opened. As we walked in we were greeted by Holland's mother, Aleta, and her six-month-old brother, Dallin. We were then introduced to Bryan, Holland's father, then to a small girl on the couch. To be honest, my first impression was, *Wow, she's tiny.* There she was, not even weighing fifty pounds—little Holland, curled up on the couch playing a game on an iPad. Like I said, she's small, pretty pale, but I could just sense the fire that was burning within

140

her. Holland is three years old and since June 1, 2012, Holland has undergone four surgeries, endless MRIs (which she has to be sedated for), and is on her second month of chemo out of twelve-month regiment. Holland's battle started nine months ago in May of 2012. She began complaining about having a headache. When the headache became a constant, and throwing up a regular occurrence, Aleta and Bryan thought it was time to take Holland to the doctors. While at their pediatrician, an MRI was conducted, and Bryan and Aleta were told to go to Primary Children's Hospital immediately.

Without any explanation as to why, the Youngs raced to Primary Children's where they were told surgery would be conducted first thing in the morning. Holland had a brain tumor the size of a golf ball as well as a cyst growing on her cerebellum. That would explain the headaches and nausea. The surgery was done, but because of the size of the masses, a second surgery would have to be done the following day to remove the remainder of the tumor. After an MRI was done, there was still a small remaining piece of the tumor in Holland's brain. At this point, Holland was fed up with hospitals, doctors, needles, feeding tubes—all the fun stuff that comes along with cancer. Bryan told me one time Holland took on four male nurses and put up a stellar fight. The Youngs decided to hold off on anything until August. There was a chance the remaining pieces would go away on their own. That July of 2012 Holland's baby brother Dallin was born.

A follow-up MRI was conducted. The fragments of tumor were still there, and a third surgery was done. While what was thought to be removed was the tumor, they were wrong. Rather, scar tissue was removed. A final fourth surgery was done and the final fragments were gone. The Youngs were relieved. Nothing was to be done now until February. Things were finally starting to look up.

This past December though, things started to become uneasy at the home front. Holland was complaining once again of headaches. Aleta didn't want to jump to any conclusions and waited to see how things played out. The instant Holland started throwing up though, back to Primary Children's Hospital they went. An MRI was done, and this time two masses were found. One the size of a quarter, and the other the size of a small orange. There was also a small mass in the brain matter. Chemo began immediately once a week and now has tapered off to once every few weeks. Holland is now in month two out of twelve of chemo. And for anyone who has been through chemo or seen it with their own eyes, we know twelve months can be . . . well it can be trying and difficult. As well as nauseating, draining, exhausting, and every other negative emotion that could come to my mind.

Amidst all this chaos and catastrophe though, never in a million years would I have guessed that Holland would have been through so much suffering. Watching her today she had energy. She was all over the room, playing games on the iPad. She was oozing with emotion as she would win and lose. You couldn't miss the smile and excitement when she downloaded a new game. Bryan also told me she had a nice follow-through and jump shot as well. Just being in the presence of this little warrior, I felt inspired. I fed off her strength and in this young girl I couldn't help but see myself. She was sassy, stubborn, and you could tell she knew she wasn't going to lose this fight.

Why do I tell you this story? Because just like me, Holland is fighting an uphill battle that requires support. Support not just from family, but from friends, and from strangers who care. I remember during my fight the amount of support I received from not just the state of Utah, but from this nation as well as other countries. It was amazing. So, in an effort to help Holland out, this Saturday there will be a fund-raiser at the Vivint gym from 10:30 to 12:00 where a Zumbathon will be held. It's eight dollars at the door and all proceeds will go to Holland and her fight with cancer.

Now, if I were you. I would come to this on Saturday. I will be there. Along with my whole family. Holland and her family, and hopefully a huge community of people, will be there. There will be a special performance at 11:00 from some members of the BYU football team, which will be entertaining I can promise that. My heart goes out to the Young family and to Holland. But after spending the afternoon with that little girl, if anyone can beat this, it's her. As I was asking Holland what her favorite part of the hospital was, she replied, "Please, I'm just trying to play this game." That's the attitude that beats cancer. The stubborn, focused, feisty ones. I hope to see some of you Saturday and we can get our dance on at Vivint (also where I work) and help raise some money for this little girl. Stay tuned for an update on my latest appointment as well! Thank you all.

Love,
Alexis

Alexis Kaufusi, "Holland Young's Battle," Alexis's Battle (blog), February 21, 2013, alexiskaufusi.blogspot.com/2013/02/holland-youngs-battle.html.

Appendix D

Spanish Fork Club Organizes 5k to Help Family with Medical Bills

Shannon Poulsen

Just before Holland Young's third birthday, she began complaining to her parents of her head hurting. The pain was keeping her up at night and making her very ill during the day. After the headaches continued to worsen, Bryan and Aleta Young decided to take their daughter to the doctor. An MRI found a golf ball-sized tumor in her brain. Within a few months, Holland endured two life-threatening surgeries to have the tumor removed. Holland, happy and energetic, recovered quickly and seemed to be back to herself again soon. In the following months things seemed to be going pretty well.

"Our faith as a family really grew and continues to," Bryan Young said. "She is such a tough little girl and such a fighter."

In December, seven months later, Holland began to complain again about having headaches. Her parents received the news that they never wanted to hear—her tumor was back and was even more aggressive. To save Holland's life, her tiny little three-year-old body would have to endure three more surgeries.

Holland is now receiving chemotherapy treatments and is doing as well as can be expected, even with the side effects from the treatments. Holland gets through the hard days by relying on her dad to give her priesthood blessings and by praying that angels will help her pain. Brian and Aleta rely on their faith and the support of family and friends.

"If you were to see Holland, you would never know anything is wrong with her besides her hair thinning a little from the chemotherapy," Aleta Young said. "She is truly an angel and through all this our family has some sacred experiences that we hold dear to us."

Nancy Miramontes, a school psychologist for Nebo School District and a close family friend of the Youngs, wanted to help her friends during this time. Knowing how expensive medical treatment was, she decided to help them pay for it. To do that, she turned to her students, the Latinos in Action at Spanish Fork High School. They opted to plan a 5K.

"I shared Holland's story with my students and they immediately began asking how as a group they could help," Miramontes said. "They have been working so hard preparing for this 5K and are so excited to help the family."

This is the second year the club has reached out to help a family in need that has an ill child.

"I know there are a lot of children who are ill in this world, but if we can help even one, we are making a difference," club member Amy Gomez said. "I felt an instant connection with Holland since we have been planning this event and I have not even ever met her."

The goal is to raise up to six thousand dollars to give to the Youngs to help with medical expenses.

Bryan was always the one on the other side helping people in need and to now be the recipient is a humbling experience. Even though the family is insured, the out-of-pocket costs for the unexpected medical bills have wiped out their savings.

"This will not only help us now but also in the future with medical bills," Bryan Young said. "Holland will continue to have doctor's visits, which will add up."

The students have been working hard to organize the 5K run, which will be held on April 13 at 8:00 a.m. at the Spanish Fork High School stadium track. They have been making signs, getting donations from local businesses, and selling wristbands with Holland's name on them for two dollars each. These bracelets can be purchased now at the finance office at SFHS and also will be available the day of the event.

"It is neat to see how many people have reached out to help us," said Rafael Gonzales, a LIA club member. "I want to help so that Holland can get the help she needs to move forward and have a normal and healthy life, like a little girl her age should."

Early registration is going on now until March 31 and for a fifteen dollar registration fee it includes a spot in the race and a shirt. If you register the day of the race it will be twenty dollars.

Holland's favorite show is "Wreck-It Ralph," so each participant's shirt will have Ralph on the front with his or her race number on the back. There will be a huge party to welcome the runners at the finish line complete with music, dancing, food, and fun.

All proceeds from the run will go to the Young Family. If you cannot run, but would like to make a donation, please send it to Spanish Fork High School, Attn: Nancy Miramontes Hope for Holland, 99 N. 300 West, Spanish Fork, UT 84660. For more information, visit sfhs.nebo.edu/ or call the school at (801) 798-4060.

Shannon Poulsen, "Spanish Fork Club Organizes 5K to Help Family with Medical Bills," *Daily Herald*, March 28, 2013, www.heraldextra.com.

Appendix E

Hope for Holland: 5K for Provo Child Battling Brain Cancer

Daniella Subieta

A 5K race called Hope for Holland will be held on April 13 to raise money for a Provo family whose three-year-old is undergoing chemotherapy after having multiple surgeries to remove brain tumors.

The usually spunky and sassy Holland Young was vomiting multiple times a day, and severe headaches kept her awake at night starting in May 2012. After several pediatrician visits and a hospital visit, an MRI revealed a golf ball-sized tumor and an equal-sized cyst attached at the back of Holland's brain.

Bryan and Aleta Young, Holland's parents, said though this was a difficult time, they learned a lot. While Holland was prepping for surgery, Bryan drove from Primary Children's Hospital in Salt Lake City back to their Provo home to get supplies for their hospital stay. Aleta, who was thirty-three weeks pregnant at the time, stayed in the hospital with Holland. Bryan said the first night after the MRI was one of the hardest.

"The drive from Salt Lake City to Provo in the middle of the night, alone with my thoughts, was really tough," Bryan Young said. "I cried the whole way home. When I got home I couldn't sleep. I was too upset and angry at God."

The next morning he went to the Provo Utah Temple.

Appendix E

"I left the temple and headed back to the hospital that day with such great peace that she may die from this, but it didn't matter because Christ had overcome death and she would live again. . . . I now know that if the Lord had healed her . . . we never would have had the opportunity to share the knowledge of the power of the Atonement with as many as people as we have," Bryan Young said.

The initial surgery was followed by four more surgeries because fragments of the tumor remained. After the fourth surgery in August, Holland was declared tumor-free. The family's elation was not to last, however, when Holland's headaches and vomiting returned in December. Another MRI revealed a new tumor, benign, but more volatile and likely to grow back and become malignant.

"This was tough on us as a family," Bryan Young said, "because we had spent the last four months thinking that everything was done. . . . I felt like all the prayer and faith we and our friends and family had exercised was not being heard, [but] the Lord taught me that our faith had been what had kept her alive and allowed her to recover so well."

The fifth surgery successfully removed the whole tumor.

Holland now receives monthly chemo treatments and will continue to do so until the end of next year to ensure the tumors do not return.

"It's really a matter of killing every last tumor cell," Holland's mother, Aleta Young, said. "But chemo certainly has its risks, . . . but we're hopeful that the chemo will wipe out any remaining tumor cells and that she goes on to lead a normal life."

Although they have health insurance, the family spent about ten thousand dollars on medical bills this year.

"This is quite a bit of money on an educator's salary," Bryan Young said. "We were fortunate because we were saving to buy a house soon, and so we had quite a bit saved up. But the costs, even with the insurance, wiped out all of our savings."

The community has responded to the Young family's predicament by joining for the upcoming 5K. The Latinos in Action class at Spanish Fork High School heard about Holland from their teacher Nancy Miramontes, a close friend of the Young family. Miramontes said the class was excited to help.

"Every one of my [students] was touched by her story," she said, "and there was no question that we wanted to find a way to make a real difference for this family."

To help, the class sold yellow silicone wristbands with Holland's name on them. The high school students, she said, are buying the wristbands, registering for the race, and making donations to the main office.

"The kids at Spanish Fork High School have really joined together to show their support for Holland. . . . It has all been very touching. Teenagers have more power and influence than we often give them credit for," Miramontes said.

The money from the 5K will help pay for chemo treatments, future medical expenses, and the family's savings so they can look again into buying a house.

"We treat the proceeds of this race like sacred funds," Bryan Young said. "It's hard to be the recipient of such generosity when we know that there are so many other people with similar trials, but the Lord has continued to bless our family."

The 5K will take place Saturday, April 13, at 8:00 a.m. at Spanish Fork High School. Online registration ends March 31. On-site registration at the high school ends at 7:45 a.m. the day of the race. Early registration is fifteen dollars (+ a two dollar service fee), and day-of is twenty dollars.

Online registration will be active from March 8 to March 31. Online registration is fifteen dollars (+ a two dollar service fee) and includes a shirt.

Daniella Subieta, "Hope for Holland: 5K for Provo Child Battling Brain Cancer," *The Daily Universe*, March 28, 2013, universe.byu.edu.

About the Author

Bryan Young is originally from Northern Virginia, but has lived in Utah since returning from his LDS mission to Boise, Idaho. He attended school at Brigham Young University where he met his wife, the former Aleta Grant. Aleta and Bryan were able to graduate at the same time in geography and psychology respectively. Bryan remained at BYU for graduate school, receiving a masters in school psychology.

Their daughter Holland was born shortly before Bryan started his career with the Provo City School District, where he is still employed as a school psychologist. They are now the parents of four children: Holland, Dallin, Nelson, and Hinckley. They currently live in Springville, Utah. Bryan enjoys BYU sports, running, playing the guitar, writing music, and pop culture trivia. Bryan looks for any opportunity to share his testimony and is grateful for every chance he has to share his daughter's story and to help other people. Learn more about Bryan and his family at meantforheaven.com.

Scan to visit

meantforheaven.com